Where Jesus Walked

5/07

Mom,
Thank you for everything!
Happy Mother's Day!
Love always,
Brett

Where Jesus Walked

A SPIRITUAL JOURNEY THROUGH THE HOLY LAND

R. WAYNE STACY

Judson Press
Valley Forge

Where Jesus Walked
A Spiritual Journey through the Holy Land

Map illustrations by Susan Bell.

Library of Congress Cataloging-in-Publication Data

Stacy, R. Wayne.
Where Jesus walked : a spiritual journey through the Holy Land / R. Wayne Stacy.
p. cm.
Includes bibliographic references.
ISBN 0-8170-1390-3 (alk. paper)
1. Jesus Christ—Biography. 2. Bible. N.T. Gospels—Geography. 3. Christian life. I. Title.
BT301.2 .S33 2001
225.9'1—dc21 00-064358

Printed in the U.S.A.

07 06 05 04 03 02 01

10 9 8 7 6 5 4 3 2 1

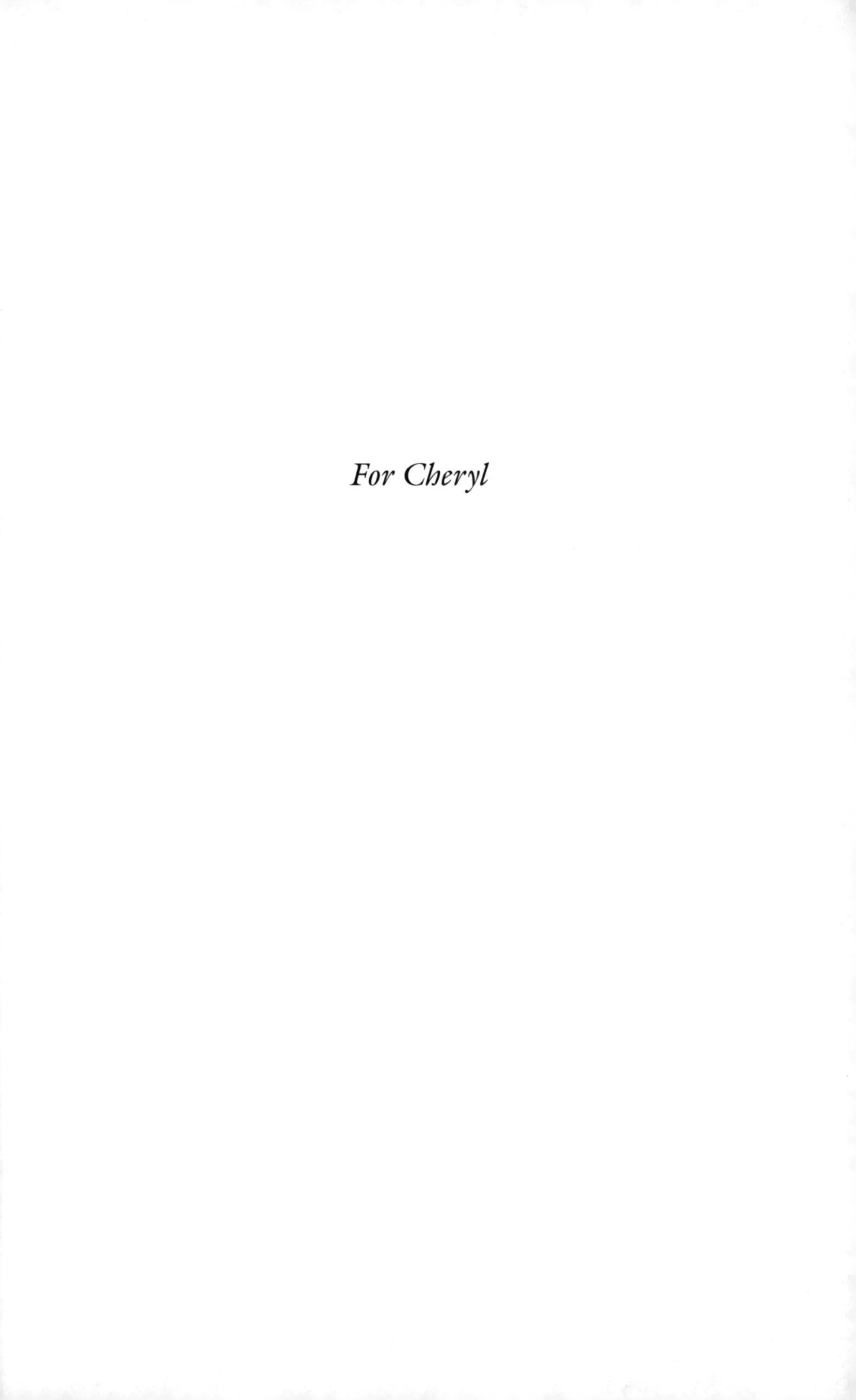

For Cheryl

Photo credits:

Pages ii-iii: Rev. John S. Mraz/St. Thomas More, Allentown, Pa.
Pages 2-3: Superstock. Pages 12-13: Dave Bartruff/Corbis. Pages 28-29: Superstock. Pages 40-41: Index Stock. Pages 50-51: Superstock.
Pages 62-63: Superstock. Pages 76-77: Superstock. Pages 90-91: Superstock.
Pages 100-101: T. Klassen Photography. Pages 120-121: Richard T. Nowitz/Corbis. Pages 138-139: Index Stock. Pages 150-151: Richard T. Nowitz/Corbis. Pages 166-167: Dave Bartruff/Corbis. Pages 174-175: Index Stock.
End pages: Rev. John S. Mraz/St. Thomas More, Allentown, Pa.

CONTENTS

INTRODUCTION

For years I have led groups of students/pilgrims to the Holy Land. You would think that by now I would be used to it—the responses of amazed and astonished people who look out in disbelief at Palestinian vistas about which they had read and heard but never seen until that moment. Typically, there is a skeptic along, someone who protests the idolatry of place that regards this land as uniquely "holy."

"Well, you can worship God anywhere. There's nothing 'holy' about this land as opposed to any other land. God is everywhere, and every land is 'holy land.'"

And it's true! God is everywhere, and the Incarnation means, among other things, that every land is "holy land," now that Jesus has walked and eaten and slept and died on it.

But then, slowly, imperceptibly at first, this place that Walter Brueggemann simply called The Land[1] does its thing, works its magic, and before they know it even the skeptics find themselves "lost in wonder, love, and praise." I have stood there and watched them become immobilized by the presence of God on the lake Jesus called Gennesaret. I have witnessed a kind of spiritual paralysis in the Garden Tomb as the curious became, in spite of themselves, captured by a place whose power over them they could neither deny nor evade.

It is a long journey from the States to the Holy Land, but not nearly as long as the journey from head to heart. It is one matter to know a thing, but it is another matter altogether to *know* a thing. And somehow, in ways fraught with mystery, faith needs a place to nourish and nurture it from nascency to maturity. I had studied the Bible all my life; I had taught it in college and seminary. I knew the history of God's self-revelation through the people of Israel and through Jesus of Nazareth as well as anyone. But when I made my first trip to the Holy Land, I discovered that I had to learn all over again what I didn't know that I didn't know. And now, I read the Bible with new eyes.

For reasons none of us can fathom, God chose this place among all places as the one in which to move from idea and feeling to bone and sinew. That God would be born at all is outrageous. And yet, once upon a time, long ago and far away, a baby who was "very God of very God," as one creed says, lay in the crook of a woman's arm, born with a skull so small you could crush it one-handed, as a contemporary believer once put it.[2] That this baby would be born in this place and not some other place is at best a curiosity, at worst a scandal. In fact, that's precisely what the scholars call it: the "scandal of particularity." But that this place reveals something of the ineffable mystery that is God as nowhere else in the world is outrageous. And yet, that is what the Bible claims. It describes a God who became incarnate, "fleshed in," as it were, at a particular time, in a particular place, rather than some nebulous, universal idea or concept not delimited to a particular moment in history. That is to say, there is a geography of revelation as well as a history of revelation. And once you have experienced the geography of revelation, "God's geography," if you will, you will never read the history of revelation in quite the same way.

The reason this is so, I think, is accessibility. We have access to the geography of revelation in a way in which we do not have access to the history of revelation. Faith needs access to its object, and though I cannot travel back in time, I can go to the place. And once I have been to the place, distance in time somehow seems less an obstacle to faith.

Indeed, some things Jesus says in the Gospels make no sense anywhere else in the world but in this place. For example, in Mark's Gospel (11:20–25) Jesus and the disciples, staying in Bethany, probably with their friends Mary, Martha, and Lazarus (cf. Luke 10:38–42), shuttle back and forth from Bethany and Bethphage over the Mount of Olives down through the Kidron Valley to Jerusalem, where Jesus daily engages his critics in the temple. On his first such visit, Jesus "cleansed" the temple, creating quite a stir by overturning the tables of the money-changers and merchandisers and pronouncing a curse on a fig tree because it did not bear fruit. The two actions were related: the temple, like the fig tree, stood "cursed" by Jesus because it too was not "bearing fruit"; that is, not doing what it was intended to do in bringing persons to God. On the next day, Jesus, with his disciples in tow, passed the fig tree he had cursed the previous day, and the disciples noticed that it had withered away at its roots (again, a parable of what would happen to the temple). And Jesus, sensing here a teachable moment, said to his disciples something that has puzzled commentators for years: "Have the faith of God. Amen, I tell you, that if you say to this mountain, 'Be taken up and cast into the sea,' and you do not doubt in your heart, but believe that what you say will happen, it will be [done] for you" (Mark 11:22–23).

And the commentators speculate about why Jesus used the image of moving mountains and casting them into the sea in order to illustrate the capacity of faith. Why would anyone want to throw a mountain into the sea? Was it just oriental hyperbole? No, it wasn't. Remember that, according to Mark, Jesus said this on his way from Bethany to the temple in Jerusalem. The path, still walked today by Palm Sunday pilgrims, takes you over the Mount of Olives, at the summit of which, on a clear day, you can see both the Herodian to the south and the Dead Sea to the east, with the temple mount lying off to the west, directly across the Kidron Valley from you. The Herodian was the tomb of Herod the Great, which Herod had built by excavating one mountain and using the excavated material to build another—his Herodian. At the time, it was regarded as such a feat of engineering that it was said of Herod that he could literally "move mountains." And Jesus, standing on the Mount of Olives, looking at Herod's mountain, uses it as an on-site object lesson and says, in effect, to his disciples, "You think that's great? That's nothing. If you have the faith of God, you can say to Herod's mountain, 'Be taken up and cast into the Dead Sea,' and it will be as you've said." Standing in that place, and only in that place, Jesus' seemingly nonsensical statement suddenly makes perfect sense.

So significant is the geography of revelation for understanding the history of revelation that Benedictine archaeologist Father Bargil Pixner likens the Land to a kind of "fifth Gospel." Reading the four Gospels in light of the fifth Gospel makes them come alive in a way in which they could not have otherwise.

And that is the purpose of this book—to lead you to reflect with me on the places "where Jesus walked" as a kind of fifth Gospel. Each chapter begins by introducing you to one of the places that, according to the four

Gospels, figured prominently in Jesus' life. A description of the geography, topography, history, and archaeology of the site is followed by a new translation (my own) of a Scripture passage depicting the event in the life of Jesus that occurred there or reflecting on some other event in Jesus' life on which this particular place sheds light. Finally, a brief meditation follows in which I reflect on the meaning of the passage for faith today. And so each chapter utilizes the same sequence: scene, Scripture, story.

My hope is that these stories from the places "where Jesus walked" will be helpful to professors, students, pastors, Sunday school teachers, and laypersons, both those who have been to the Holy Land and those who have not; that is, for pilgrims both real and virtual. For one who is leading a tour to the Holy Land, these descriptions and stories can be used for spiritual reflection and stimulation as you stand with your group on these sites and feel Jesus' power and presence in these places. For those who have not yet been to the Holy Land, perhaps a better insight into the life and ministry of Jesus can be had vicariously as you stand with me in these places where he stood and listen in on echoes of conversations long ago and far away. In either case, it is my fervent hope that through the insights we gain from having walked "where Jesus walked" you will be able to understand a little better why so many of us continue to call this Land "holy."

Special thanks must be expressed to several persons who assisted me with this project. Randy Frame, of Judson Press, was helpful and encouraging in bringing this project to press. My administrative assistant, Becky Newton, cheerfully assisted me with the myriad details involved in a project such as this. My president and Middle East travel partner, Chris White, offered encouragement and helpful critical insight during the writing. My colleague and friend, Robert Canoy, provided invaluable critical commentary on the manuscript before it went to press. Finally, in everything I do, my wife, Cheryl, is my most valued colleague and trusted friend. Without her help, I would never do anything very well.

NOTES

1. Walter Brueggemann, *The Land: Place as Gift, Promise, and Challenge in Biblical Faith* (Philadelphia: Fortress Press, 1977).

2. Frederick Buechner, *Whistling in the Dark: An ABC Theologized* (San Francisco: Harper & Row, 1988), 29.

Part I

Galilee

CHAPTER 1

Nazareth: The Church of the Annunciation

Nazareth was Jesus' hometown. Both Matthew and Luke report that Jesus grew up in Nazareth.[1] According to Matthew, Joseph returned to Nazareth following the flight to Egypt rather than settling in Judea, where Jesus was born, because Archelaus, who ruled Judea when his father, Herod the Great, died in 4 BCE, proved to be just as unpredictable as his murderous father had been, making Judea unsafe for Joseph and his family (Matthew 2:22). Moreover, Herod the Great's other son, Herod Antipas, who had become ruler of Galilee upon his father's death, had just made Sepphoris, a city about four miles from Nazareth and situated on the Roman road to Jerusalem, his capital and was recruiting stone masons, artisans, and carpenters for its construction. Hence, Joseph, a carpenter who could support his family by working in nearby Sepphoris, settled his family in Nazareth in the relative safety of the Galilee.

But why Nazareth? Why not just live in Sepphoris, closer to his work? Typically, Matthew's answer is to quote the Scripture: "so that the word spoken through the prophets, 'He shall be called a Nazarene,' might be fulfilled" (2:23). But there's more here than just a proof text. The reference is to Isaiah 11:1, "A rod will come up from the stump of Jesse; from his roots a shoot [*netzer*] will bear fruit." The word *netzer*, from which the name Nazareth derives, means "shoot" of Jesse, or descendant of David. The entire village of Nazareth was comprised of returnees from the Exile who were descendants *(netzerim)* of David; that is, Nazarenes. And so Joseph, himself a *netzer*, made Nazareth his home. And Jesus, though he was born in Bethlehem, would call Nazareth his "hometown."

The Nazareth of today is a bustling Arab city of over sixty thousand inhabitants, the majority of whom are Muslim or Christian. Nestled in the hills of Galilee some 1,230 feet above sea level and overlooking the Jezreel Valley, the

Nazareth of today bears little resemblance to the village that was the home of the Davidic clan of Jesus' day. The Nazareth of Jesus' day probably had fewer than two hundred residents, most of whom were members of Jesus' extended family ("kinfolk," *syngeneis*, as Mark 6:4 calls them). Ascending to Nazareth from the Jezreel Valley, you pass on your right the Mount of Precipation, which, according to tradition, was the place from which Jesus' kinfolk, angry at the implications of his first sermon there in the Nazareth synagogue, tried to throw him to his death.[2]

Modern Nazareth is dominated by the Church of the Annunciation, situated in the heart of the city and visible from almost anywhere. Dedicated in 1968, the church was constructed over the ancient site of a pre-Byzantine Jewish-Christian synagogue, some of which can still be seen in the lower church beneath the contemporary structure. From 1955 to 1960, the Franciscans excavated the site, revealing a series of grottoes, silos, cisterns, mosaic floors, graffiti, and *mikvaoth* (Jewish ritual baths). The archaeological discoveries are not from the time of Jesus, but they do give evidence of an early Jewish-Christian veneration of the site, suggesting that from as early as the second century this place was commemorated as the place "where Jesus grew up." It is almost certainly the place visited by the anonymous Christian known as the Pilgrim of Piacenza (570 CE), who wrote of the site, "We traveled on to the city of Nazareth, where many miracles take place. In the synagogue there is kept the book in which the Lord wrote his ABC's, and in this synagogue is the bench on which he sat with the other children."[3] The church now fully covers what was once the entire village complex of Nazareth in Jesus' day, including the synagogue that served as Jesus' elementary school and "home church." It was, no doubt, a place that brought him much joy—and great grief.

The Scripture: Luke 4:16–30

And he came to Nazareth, where he had been brought up, and he entered according to his custom on the sabbath day into the synagogue and stood up to read. And the scroll of the prophet Isaiah was given to him, and he unrolled the scroll and found the place where it stands written:

> The Spirit of the Lord is upon me,
> in behalf of which he has anointed me
> to proclaim good news to the poor.
> He has sent me
> to proclaim release to captives
> and recovery of sight to the blind,
> to send forth the traumatized in release,
> to proclaim the year of the Lord's favor.

And having rolled up the scroll and having given it back to the attendant, he sat down. And all eyes in the synagogue were transfixed on him. And he began to say to them, "Today this scripture is fulfilled in your hearing."

And all were bearing witness to him and were amazed at the words of grace that proceeded from his mouth, and they were saying, "Is this not Joseph's son?"

And he said to them, "Truly you will speak to me this parable, 'Physician, heal yourself; as many things as we have heard have happened in Capernaum do also here in your hometown.'"

And he said, "Amen, I say to you: No prophet is favorably received in his hometown. And for a truth I tell you, there were many widows in Israel in the days of Elijah, when the heavens were shut up for three years and six months, as there was a great famine over all the land. And to not even one of them was Elijah sent except Zarephath of Sidon, to the widow woman. And there were many lepers in Israel in the time of Elisha the prophet, and not one of them was cleansed except Naaman the Syrian."

And they were all filled with rage in the synagogue hearing these things, and having arisen, they cast him out of the city and led him to the precipice upon which their city was built so that they might throw him down to his death. But passing through the middle of them, he kept right on going on his way.

"The Sermon"

First sermons are nerve-racking affairs for everyone involved. I remember my first sermon. I was sixteen years old when I felt "the call" and "surrendered" to the ministry, as we used to describe it in rural Baptist life. That word "surrender" was a pretty heavy term in those days. Typically, it was accompanied with heart-wrenching, down-and-dirty stories of the minister fleeing from God, only to be hunted down by God's call, ultimately leading to the minister's "surrender" to the ministry. Hearing those stories, and not having had any personal "far country" experience upon which to draw, I remember feeling slightly embarrassed that I had not put up more of a struggle.

But once I had gone public, it was inevitable that sooner or later I would have to preach my first sermon. They don't call you "preacher" in Baptist life for nothing.

Well, the dreaded day dawned. My pastor asked me to preach on a Sunday night. I worked for weeks on that sermon. My subject was a modest one: "God, Mankind, the Universe, and Other Related Subjects." I had practiced my sermon in front of the mirror. Somebody told me I should do that. Unfortunately, the person who told me that wasn't a preacher, and my practiced mannerisms showed. My gestures were hopelessly artificial.

"Now I have three [holding up three fingers] things I want to say tonight about God. The first is, God is Big." Dramatic pause for effect. I had seen that done before.

"The second is, God is Good."

"The third is, God is the Ontological Ground of Our Being with Whom We Must Existentially Interact." I had found a book in the library.

Needless to say, that night was not one of the high points of my preaching career. Indeed, when I got to the seminary, very first class, the professor began to call the roll: "John Archer, William Barber, Charles Crane, Frank Sanders, Wayne Stacy," and then he paused, looked down over his glasses, and said, "Heard about your sermon, Stacy." It was a painful memory.

But no matter how difficult an experience my first sermon was, it pales in comparison to Jesus'. At least my audience didn't try to take me out and stone me to death, no matter how richly I may have deserved it.

What really happened that day in Nazareth? What turned those good, churchgoing folk into a lynch mob?

As Luke describes it, that Sabbath service started out typically enough. Jesus, the hometown "preacher boy" who had made good, returned to his "home church" to worship. Being a guest "preacher," rabbi, he was invited, as was the custom, to come to the lectern and read the *haftarah,* the prophetic passage for the day. The text was from Isaiah 61, a well-known passage that heralded the hope that one day Israel, on the far side of the Exile, would once again experience God's blessing and favor. When he finished reading, he gave the scroll back to the attendant and, after the fashion of Jewish rabbis, sat down to preach the sermon on the text he'd just read. Luke reports that the congregation's initial response to Jesus' words was positive, but soon began to sour (Luke 4:22–23). Then, although he does not give us the entire sermon Jesus preached that day, he supplies for us two of the stories, sermon illustrations, Jesus told.

It's fairly safe to say that the sermon was not a "hit." They dragged Jesus out to the precipice of the hill on which Nazareth sat to throw him down to be stoned to death. What happened between "and they all spoke well of him and marveled at the words of grace that came from his mouth" and "they rose up and put him out of the city, and led him away to be stoned"?

The sermon happened! Luke doesn't want us to miss it. He rivets our attention to the sermon: "and all eyes in the synagogue were transfixed on him."

Now, we know why. Thanks to the Dead Sea Scrolls, we now know that this passage, Isaiah 61, was the favorite text of Jews in first-century occupied Palestine, because it spoke about a great reversal of fortunes: God would restore Israel to its former glory and visit judgment and destruction upon Israel's oppressors.[4]

No wonder, then, that "they all spoke well of him" when he finished reading the text and announced, "Today this scripture has been fulfilled in your hearing."

"Boy, don't you just love his preaching! I can't believe this is his first sermon. We've got ourselves a good one here."

And then the other shoe drops. Jesus tells two stories, the point of both being that God doesn't divide the world into "friend or foe" as we do. All people, including those we would call enemies, are God's people. The "good news" that Jesus has come to proclaim is just that—good news, not good news for some and bad news for others.

When the sermon was over, Luke says, the congregation, having gotten the point, became indignant. And they looked at one another and said, "I hate his preaching. Just who does he think he is, coming in here like that and trying to tell us about our God!"

It was the sermon that set them off—make no mistake about it. Jesus, standing in the great prophetic tradition, was doing what prophets always do: reminding them, and us, the "chosen people," that God is God, and is free to do whatever, with whomever, God pleases, whether that pleases us or not.

And that's so hard to hear, because it's just a short step from saying "I am God's" to saying "God is mine." Once we've experienced God's grace, our human propensity is to become proprietary with it and reserve it only for "our kind." But the gospel, the "good news," is that because God is God and is Father of us all, all kinds are God's kind, and that means that all kinds are "our kind." That is good news, isn't it?

That's what happened that day in the synagogue there at Nazareth, when a bunch of good, churchgoing folk turned into a lynch mob and tried to stone one of their own kinfolk to death. But the gospel has that kind of power over people—to terrorize or to transform. I know, you see, because as I sat there that day in the synagogue listening to the sermon, I looked down, and there in my hand was a stone.

For Further Discussion

1. What is the significance of the fact that early Christians called Jesus a "Nazarene"?
2. Why does Luke say that most of the people who heard Jesus the day he preached in the synagogue at Nazareth were his "kinfolk"?
3. What was the significance of the text Jesus read from Isaiah to first-century Jews?
4. What was there about Jesus' sermon that made the Jewish synagogue worshipers indignant?
5. Do you find it significant that the very first threat to Jesus' life came not from the Romans (pagans) but from his own hometown synagogue, populated, as the New Testament says, "with his own kin"?
6. In your judgment, from where does the greatest threat to the gospel come today?

NOTES

1. Matthew and Luke disagree over whether Joseph and Mary lived in Nazareth prior to Jesus' birth. Luke says that they did (2:4–5), while Matthew implies that they didn't (2:23). The story of the annunciation by the angel Gabriel to Mary informing her that she would bear the Christ is Lukan (1:26–38), hence, the traditions about the place of the annunciation gathered around Nazareth rather than Judea. For a fuller treatment of this issue, see Bargil Pixner, *With Jesus through Galilee* (Rosh Pina, Israel: Corazin Publishing, 1992), 13–24.

2. In the first century, you stoned someone in one of two ways. Either you threw stones at the person, or you threw the person at the stones. The people of Nazareth were attempting to stone Jesus by employing the second method.

3. Cited in Jerome Murphy-O'Connor, *The Holy Land: An Archaeological Guide from Earliest Times to 1700,* rev. ed. (New York: Oxford University Press, 1986), 310.

4. See James A. Sanders, "From Isaiah 61 to Luke 4," in *Christianity, Judaism, and Other Greco-Roman Cults: Studies for Morton Smith at Sixty,* vol. 1, *New Testament,* ed. Jacob Neusner (Leiden: E. J. Brill, 1975), 75–106.

CHAPTER 2

Cana of Galilee: The Church of the Wedding

About five miles due north of Nazareth is the little village of Cana, or Kefr Kenna. On the ancient road from Nazareth to Capernaum, Kefr Kenna is one of two places vying for the claim to be the site where, according to John, Jesus performed the first miracle of turning water into wine (John 2:1–11). The other claimant is a village much farther to the north, known as Khirbet Khana. The former has the support of tradition, the latter of scholars. Neither is beyond dispute.

In favor of Kefr Kenna is that this little village is near Nazareth (a few hours' walk); it lies on the major road from Nazareth to Capernaum (from Kefr Kenna the path leads downward through Wadi Hamam, Arabic for the "Valley of the Doves," straight to the shore of the Sea of Galilee and the Via Maris to Capernaum); and discovered there was a mosaic with ancient Aramaic writing that seems to indicate that, early on, the site housed a Jewish-Christian synagogue. This mosaic is displayed in the chapel's narthex.

In favor of Khirbet Khana is that from the twelfth century onward, pilgrims seem to have venerated this site as the place of the miracle of the wine.[1] Moreover, the Arabic name Khana is closer to the word "Cana" than is Kenna, it being difficult to explain the double *n* in Kenna. Against the location of Khirbet Khana, however, is that in Jesus' day Khirbet Khana was not located in the Galilee, but in Asher, nearer to Tyre and Sidon in the territory of ancient Phoenicia, far out of the way to travel for Jesus to perform his first miracle when he left Nazareth for the Sea of Galilee and Capernaum. Add to this that according to John, Jesus' mother, Mary, traveled with him to the wedding, and the site of Khirbet Khana seems all the more improbable. For these reasons, clerics and pilgrims alike prefer the Kefr Kenna site as the original.

Today, Kefr Kenna is a small Arab village (mostly Christian). Situated in an idyllic setting of olive groves, cultivated grape vineyards, and fig trees, two rival churches (Roman Catholic and Greek Orthodox) both claim to be the "Church of the Wedding." The better known and most visited by pilgrims and tourists is the Franciscan (Roman Catholic) Church of the Wedding. Built in the late-nineteenth century, the church is a simple and elegant chapel commemorating the wedding at which Jesus first revealed his extraordinary powers and personage. In the front of the chapel hangs a painting that commemorates and celebrates Jesus' miracle of the wine. You will notice in the painting the artist's depiction of the stone water jars containing the Jewish purification water that, according to John's account, Jesus used to produce the wine (a not-so-subtle symbol that the "new wine" that Jesus brought into the world superseded the "old water" of Judaism). Beneath the present chapel a grotto is preserved that, according to the Franciscans, is the very spot on which Jesus performed the miracle. You can reach the grotto via a set of stairs that descends into the cave beneath the church. In the grotto the Franciscans have placed a stone water jar (*lithinē hydria* in Greek, *cli* in Hebrew) that replicates the kind of large stone vessel that would have been used in Jesus' time. The jar is meant to give you some idea of how large these stone vessels really were.

Unlike contemporary Western wedding practices in which the bride is the focus, ancient Jewish wedding practices centered on the groom (cf. Mark 2:18–20, and parallels). The pattern for Jewish weddings in the first century consisted first of a wedding procession in which the bridegroom's friends brought the bride to the groom's house. Then the actual wedding ceremony took place, followed by a wedding supper or feast. It was not unusual for the festivities to last as long as a week![2] John appears to reflect this custom with his description of the "steward of the feast," or the maître d', by means of the Greek word *architriklinos*, literally, "chief of the *triclinium*." The *triclinium* (literally, "three-sided bed") was a low, three-sided table at which guests reclined on their left side in order to be able to eat with their right hand (it was considered impolite to eat with one's left hand). The *triclinium* was typically reserved for festive celebrations such as weddings and the like. John's use of the term was altogether appropriate for such an occasion and witnesses to the authenticity of the story he tells.

The presence of the stone water jars for the Jewish purification ritual also seems to reflect authentic Jewish practice in the first century and provides authenticating detail to John's account of the wedding at Cana. Pottery jars, the typical houseware of the day, would not do for a religiously important ceremony such as a wedding because the clay of pottery jars might disintegrate into the water, thereby contaminating it. Stone jars, however, would not be susceptible to such deterioration and thus were the vessels of preference for holy, ritual, and ceremonial occasions such as this.

In the same way, John's seemingly meaningless detail that the wedding occurred on the "third day" becomes significant when one realizes that in Judaism the third day of the week, Tuesday, was the preferred day for a wedding. In Israel today, it still is. When the tourist or pilgrim stays in a Jewish hotel in the Holy Land, his or her sleep will frequently be interrupted on Tuesday nights with weddings and the partying and feasting that inevitably accompany them. This is because of all the days of the week mentioned in Genesis on which God's creative activity occurred, the third day was the only one about which it was twice said, "And God saw that it was good" (cf. Genesis 1:9–13). Hence, Jews in Israel to this day regard "the third day" as the day of choice for weddings, and a wedding that takes place on a Tuesday is likewise considered "twice blessed." Of course, for John, "the third day" also has the theological import of being "resurrection day." And so, the miracle of the wine, taking place as it does on "the third day," becomes a resurrection event, a breakthrough event, an epiphany, a manifestation of who Jesus really is.

For Jesus, the miracle of the wedding wine was precisely that—a "coming out," an epiphany of the fact that he was the revelation of God in blood and flesh. Indeed, in some ancient churches (fourth century) the anniversary of the miracle of the wine, rather than the visit of the magi (Matthew 2:1–12) as in the contemporary liturgical tradition, was celebrated as the "Feast of the Epiphany."[3]

The Scripture: John 2:1–11

And on the third day a wedding occurred in Cana of Galilee, and the mother of Jesus was there. And Jesus and his disciples also were called to the wedding. And when the wine was exhausted, the mother of Jesus said to him, "They have no wine." And Jesus said to her, "What is there between you and me, woman? My hour has not yet come." And his mother said to the servants, "Whatever he should say to you, do."

Now six stone water jars were set there according to the purification [customs] of the Jews, [each] holding twenty or thirty gallons. Jesus said to them, "Fill the water jars with water"; and they filled them to the top. And he said to them, "Now draw [some] and take it to the maître d'." And they took it [to him]. But when the maître d' tasted the water having become wine, and not knowing from where it came (though the servants who drew the water knew), the maître d' called the bridegroom and said to him, "Everyone puts [on the table] first the good wine, and when everyone becomes drunk, the poorer. [But] you have kept the good wine until now!"

Jesus did this first of [his] signs in Cana of Galilee, and [thereby] manifested his glory; and his disciples believed in him.

"Epiphany"[4]

Something always goes wrong at weddings. Have you noticed that? The florist runs late; the tuxedos don't fit; the in-laws get angry; the photographer's a nut; your best friends don't show up, but your crazy uncle George does. It's not really surprising that weddings are such magnets for mishap when you consider what they really are: high church and state occasions involving amateurs under pressure. I guess it's because of sheer grace that most of them turn out as well as they do.

I guess I've done a couple of hundred weddings in my thirty-odd years of ministry, and I thought I'd seen it all. But the wedding story Robert Fulghum tells in his book *It Was on Fire When I Lay Down on It* takes the "wedding cake."[5] I warn you, those of you out there who are planning your own weddings or the weddings of your children may not want to read this.

The central figure in this wedding debacle was the mother of the bride, "MOTB" for short. This sane and intelligent woman went through an amazing transformation at the announcement of her daughter's engagement: she became unhinged. Nobody knew it, but she had been quietly waiting for this day with a script for a production that would make Cecil B. DeMille look like a rank amateur. During the seven months prior to the wedding day she checked and rechecked every possible detail of the wedding, leaving nothing to chance or human error. "Everything that could be engraved was engraved," says Fulghum.[6] The minister met with the bride and groom three times during that seven-month period—the MOTB he met with weekly! His secretary announced her visits simply by saying, "She's here." No further introduction was needed.

Well, the big day finally—and I do mean finally—arrived. Guests in formal attire packed the church. Enough candles were lit to send the fire marshal into apoplexy. And then, in all her regal splendor, the MOTB coasted down the aisle to take her seat of honor, there to view the spectacle she'd been orchestrating for seven months.

Unbeknownst to her, however, the bride was sequestered in the church fellowship hall with her father to await the big moment. Of the bride Fulghum says, "She'd been dressed for hours, if not days."[7] By this time, she was so nervous that she wasn't even sure anymore of whom it was she was marrying. Nervously, she began to walk by the tables filled with gourmet goodies for the guests and absentmindedly began to nibble away on the little pink and yellow and green mints. Then on to the mixed nuts she went, followed by the cheese balls, black olives, and glazed almonds, the little toothpick-impaled sausages and the bacon-wrapped shrimp, and finally, she finished off with a cracker piled high with liver pâté. To wash it all down, she gulped down a glass of pink champagne, which her father gave to her to calm her nerves.

When she finally arrived at the door of the church for the wedding march, what you noticed first was not her dress, but her face—it was wedding-dress white. "For what was coming down the aisle," Fulghum quips, "was not a bride, but a walking grenade with the pin pulled out."[8]

And then it happened. Just as she walked past her mother, the bride threw up. And I mean threw up, as in puked. This was no polite, ladylike indiscretion into a hanky. Oh, no. She hosed the chancel! She wasted the bridesmaids, the groom, the ring bearer, and the minister. Having disgorged her hors d'oeuvres, champagne, and the last of her dignity, the bride went limp in her father's arms, while the MOTB fainted dead away. Later, when the chaos had subsided and the bride revived, it was decided that the wedding would go on. Cecil would have wanted it that way. But when the ceremony finally got cranked up again, Fulghum remarks, only two people were seen to be smiling: the mother of the groom and the father of the bride![9]

Don't you just love weddings? All kinds of things can go wrong at weddings.

John tells about a near disaster at a wedding in Cana of Galilee. If you think weddings can be big events in our world, you should have seen the way weddings were conducted in the ancient world of first-century Judaism.

Marriage in first-century Judaism began with betrothal, *kiddushin,* which was legally binding on the couple, the betrothal ceremony culminating in the writing of a marriage contract, *ketubah,* which stipulated how the bride was acquired and when the marriage proper would occur. You will remember that Joseph, upon learning that Mary was pregnant, contemplated divorcing her. This sounds strange to us, in that they were only engaged. But among first-century Jews, the *kiddushin* was as binding as marriage. The marriage ceremony itself took place on a Tuesday if possible—the "third day," the twice-blessed day—amidst great pomp and ceremony, typically about one year after the signing of the *ketubah.*

On the great day a tent (*chapheh,* or as it is commonly called today, "chuppah") would be spread, under which the wedding ceremony was conducted. That practice is preserved today in the bridal canopy used in Jewish weddings. The canopy symbolized the "canopy of the heavens" spread out above the couple as a sign that God was present to "witness" their marriage and thus to bless it. Today, the canopy is usually sky blue to reflect the idea of the "canopy of the heavens," the *ha-shamayim* of Genesis 1. And all around the blessed occasion, both before and after the ceremony itself, was the party, the feast that the guests would enjoy with singing and dancing and eating and drinking, often continuing for the entire week.

That's why when Mary came to Jesus with the revelation "Son, we're out of wine!" the tension became palpable. You see, in an oriental culture hospitality is the most prized virtue. To run out of wine at a wedding party was a faux pas every bit as big as the one Fulghum describes in his story, because the hosts would have thereby lost face with their guests, an unthinkable shame in the oriental world.

And so Mary and Jesus have words. "Son, can't you do something?" asks Mary. And Jesus responds, "Woman, what have you to do with me? My hour has not yet come." But Mary persisted, and after a while Jesus acceded. He tells the servants to fill the six stone water jars, kept for Jewish purification rites, to the brim. Each one held about twenty or thirty gallons of water. (I told you it was a big wedding.) And quick as a flash, Jesus had turned the water into wine. When the maître d' tasted the wine, he exclaimed, "Wow! This is good stuff! I'm impressed. Hosts usually serve the good stuff first, and then when everyone gets a little tipsy, they bring out the watered-down stuff so no one will notice. But you've saved the best for last!" And John adds the epilogue: "Now this was the first of Jesus' signs."

Did you get that? John called it a "sign," *sēmeia* in the Greek. That's John's word for the miracles—"signs." That is, there's more here than meets the eye. It's his way of saying, "Don't get so hung up on the obvious miracle that you fail to see the real miracle here. Don't focus so much on what happened that you fail to see what really happened." And so he calls them "signs," breakthroughs, epiphanies in which the everyday is transformed by the eternal, the prosaic by the poetic.

This story is an "epiphany story," in which the glory of God breaks through and transforms those who see it—"and the disciples believed in him."

John makes that clear to us in two ways, one explicit, one subtle. In a direct statement John says, "This, the first of his signs, Jesus did at Cana in Galilee, and manifested his glory." But if you're reading the story carefully, you already know that this story is about more than a wine shortage. Remember, John began by telling us that the marriage happened "on the third day." As I said, Tuesday was, and is, the favorite day for Jewish weddings. But "the third day" is also a resurrection symbol, the day when new life "broke out" and "broke through."

All this is John's way of saying, "This is no ordinary wedding; it's an epiphany of the grace of God, a 'window into another world' revealing to us a miraculous new life that 'breaks through' and takes us completely by surprise."

Sometimes it happens that way, these epiphanies of the grace of God.

Isak Dinesen, which is the pseudonym of Karen Blixsen, author of *Out of Africa,* has written a marvelous short story that was made into an equally marvelous French-language film. It's called *Babette's Feast.*[10]

It's a simple story, really, worthy of Gustave Flaubert. A young French woman named Babette suffered a severe economic reversal due to political upheaval in France. Having no husband or family, she came to live in a small, rural village in Denmark with two sisters who provided Babette with room and board in exchange for her cooking and cleaning for them.

They knew very little about Babette and had no idea who she was or what she had done in France, but they needed a cook and so they graciously took her in. They meticulously taught her everything they required of her, assuming nothing. They taught her how to boil potatoes and to make a simple stew, which was about all they could afford on their meager means. Babette listened intently and followed their instructions without question. As time went by, Babette became a trusted member of the family and took care of the two elderly sisters with loyalty and devotion.

But then one day, Babette received some extraordinary news. She had come into a rather large sum of money, enough, if it were managed properly, to provide for her needs from then on. The sisters fully expected Babette to quit her employment with them and return to France, when she came to them and said, "I would like to prepare a meal for you and for your friends as an expression of my gratitude for all you've done for me. But I would like to prepare for you an authentic *French* meal, a very special feast." They assured her that it was not necessary, but Babette insisted.

She sent to France for all the ingredients for the feast and carefully prepared the meal with all the care and alacrity of the best chefs in France. When the meal was served, the sisters and their friends sat down to a sumptuous feast the likes of which they had never before seen. All except one of them. One of the sisters' friends in attendance said that this meal reminded him precisely of a feast he had enjoyed years before at one of France's greatest restaurants. He commented to the other guests, "This meal must have cost a fortune!"

After the meal, when the sisters asked Babette how she had learned to prepare such an elegant culinary experience, she told them that she had been the chef at the very restaurant in France that the guest had spoken of. All the while the sisters had patiently taught Babette how to peel potatoes, she had been one of France's greatest chefs, and not a word of protest!

The sisters said, "Well, we guess you'll go back to France now."

Babette replied, "No, I will stay here and cook for you."

"Stay here? Why would you want to stay here and cook for us—what, with all your money?"

"I have no money."

"No money? What happened to it?"

"I spent it on the feast."

"You spent it all on a meal for us?"

"Yes, I spent it all; but it wasn't just a meal. Was it?"

Sometimes, the strangest things become vehicles of the grace of God. Sometimes the strangest people do, too.

Take, for example, Ferrol Sams's character, Gregry, in his book *Epiphany.*[11] *Epiphany* is the story of a family doctor of the old school, Dr. Mark Goddard, who has become frustrated and disillusioned with the high-tech, low-touch approach to medicine that's invaded the clinic where he practices. The clinic has brought in a young turk administrator named Dennis who officiously rides herd on the physicians to make sure that they see as many patients as possible taking up as little time as possible with each, and practice their medicine not so much with a view toward helping their patients as to avoiding litigation and liability. Dr. Goddard not only detests this assembly-line approach to medicine, but also chafes at Dennis's obtrusive and bureaucratic style. He constantly rails against what he calls the "new trinity" in medicine of "Medicare, Malpractice, and Medical Records."

To "get Dennis's goat," Dr. Goddard, who loves poetry, regularly intersperses lines from A. E. Housman and Edna St. Vincent Millay and Lewis Carroll and Robert Browning throughout his "patient encounter logs" when he dictates them, knowing that the transcriptionists will notify the clinic administrator's office of this grievous breach of medical procedure, which will then send Dennis flying into Dr. Goddard's office protesting, "How would this look in a courtroom should your logs ever be subpoenaed, quoting poetry in a patient log like that!" To which old Doc Goddard responds that should Dennis stop just long enough to lift his nose out of his spreadsheets and deposit it in some of that poetry he's always railing against, he might just learn that there's more going on around him than bottom lines and patient logs.

That's about the only diversion in Dr. Goddard's otherwise drab and pedestrian life, until a new patient comes to see him, Gregry McHune—that's "Gregry" with no *o*. Ostensibly, he comes in to have his high blood pressure treated, but as he returns week after week, a strange friendship develops. In many ways, they have absolutely nothing in common: Dr. Goddard is a highly educated, extremely literate Renaissance man trapped in a system that doesn't understand him and for which he has no respect, and Gregry is a rough, red-necked, blue-collared, six-packing "good ol' boy" who's done time in the state prison for manslaughter. But as the weeks go by, Dr. Goddard spends less and less time treating Gregry and more and more time listening to him. And as he learns more and more of Gregry's story, he discovers in Gregry a human spirit struggling heroically against incredible odds to "do the right thing," and he's drawn to him like a moth to a flame.

And then a strange thing begins to happen. Goddard discovers that in this bizarre friendship with this man who seemed to have nothing at all to offer him, he is, in fact, receiving more than he's giving. He rediscovers, in the simple relationship that the brief encounters between doctor and patient afford, a renaissance, a rebirth, an epiphany, if you will, of his own life and vitality and purpose. He says to Gregry after one session in which Gregry had held him spellbound telling him of his hard and cruel life, "Gregry McHune, you are an epiphany! I am constantly amazed at the resilience of the human spirit and humbled by the manifestation of unanticipated grace."

John says that that day in Cana was the first of Jesus' signs, "and he manifested his glory." It was a biggy—turning water into wine! The disciples must have been pleased that they had chosen so well, following such a high-powered messiah. They didn't know—how could they know?—where he would ultimately take them; that things would get complicated and confused; that one day they would drink wine together one last time and Jesus would talk not of water and weddings but of body and blood, his and theirs, and the joy and jubilation of Cana would seem a faint and distant memory.

And you don't know what lies ahead for you either. But of this much you can be sure: there will be more mundane moments on your journey than glorious ones. Would that every morning held a wedding, and every night a magical midsummer night's dream. But inevitably, joy's moments give way to reality. The late night phone call: "Your child's been in an accident." The early morning diagnosis: "The tests were positive." The end-of-the-week pink slip: "I'm sorry, but we're going to have to let you go." No matter how lofty the heights or glorious the moment, sooner or later you must go back into an always pedestrian, sometimes dangerous, world where the party's over and hope is in short supply.

But as you go, remember the epiphanies—the breakthroughs, those grace-filled moments when the glory gleamed, and the real pierced the sham, and you saw it all clearly, if not fully—moments in which right in the middle of the everyday, Eternity happened, and the water became wine, and supper became sacrament, and mere community was transformed into communion.

And when the darkness returns—and it will, it will—hold on to that God who always saves the best for last, and you'll be all right.

You will!

For Further Discussion

1. Why has Tuesday (the third day of the week) remained the favored day for Jewish weddings?

2. Why was running out of wine regarded as such a crisis at the wedding in Cana?

3. How do you account for Jesus' rather curt response to his mother's request?

4. Why does John refer to Jesus' miracles as "signs"?

5. Has God worked any "signs" in your life?

NOTES

1. D. C. Pellett, "Cana," *Interpreter's Dictionary of the Bible* (Nashville: Abingdon Press, 1962), 1:493–94.

2. Raymond E. Brown, *The Gospel According to John (I–XII)* (Garden City, N.Y.: Doubleday, 1966), 97–98.

3. Jack Finegan, *The Archeology of the New Testament: The Life of Jesus and the Beginning of the Early Church* (Princeton, N.J.: Princeton University Press, 1978), 66.

4. A version of this homily was first published in R. Wayne Stacy, *The Search: The Soul's Secret Signature* (Nashville: Fields Publishing, 2000), 35–40. Reprinted with permission.

5. Robert Fulghum, *It Was on Fire When I Lay Down on It* (New York: Ivy Books, 1998), 7–13.

6. Ibid., 8.

7. Ibid., 9.

8. Ibid., 10.

9. Ibid., 11.

10. Isak Dinesen, *Babette's Feast and Other Anecdotes of Destiny* (New York: Vintage Books, 1988), 3–48.

11. Ferrol Sams, *Epiphany* (New York: Penguin Books, 1994), esp. 1–119.

CHAPTER 3

The Sea of Galilee

One of the most spectacular sights in the world looms before the pilgrim's eyes on the drive from Nazareth down to the freshwater lake known in the New Testament as the Sea of Galilee. And a drive down it is, for as soon as you leave the elevated heights of the city of Nazareth, perched 1,230 feet above sea level, you begin to feel the precipitous descent of 1,926 feet to the lake's shore, where you now stand some 696 feet below sea level.

On your way, you pass by the ruins of Sepphoris, just four miles northwest of Nazareth, the city that Herod's son Antipas made his capital until 20 CE, when he replaced it with Tiberias, the city he built on the western shore of the Sea of Galilee and named for his friend Tiberias Caesar.[1] Called by the Jewish historian Josephus "the ornament of all Galilee," Sepphoris was a sophisticated, bustling, multicultural Jewish city in the first century, and must have held much fascination for the adolescent Jesus. It was also the traditional birthplace of Mary, Jesus' mother. About a mile or so past Sepphoris you come to Kefr Kenna, the village of Cana, where, according to John 2, Jesus turned water to wine at a wedding (see chapter 2). Leaving Cana, you see to the north two smallish mountains. They look unimpressive when you pass them on your way to the lake, but from the lake looking back to the west, they rise above Wadi el-Hamam like two giant horns protruding from the earth. Indeed, that's precisely what they're called, the Horns of Hattin. It was there in 1187 that the Crusaders' dominion of the Holy Land ended with an ignominious defeat at the hands of the army of the Moslem Saladin. From the Horns of Hattin down to the lake the descent is precipitous, until at last, far below, you catch sight of it: the large lake known in Jesus' time as the Sea of Gennesaret.

Thirteen miles long and seven miles wide at is widest point, the lake has a circumference of more than thirty-two miles. It takes its name, Gennesaret, from the Greek pronunciation of the Hebrew *Kinnereth* (cf. Numbers 34:11;

Joshua 12:3; 13:27), which in turn derives from the Hebrew word *kinnor,* meaning "harp" or "lyre." Indeed, the lake is harp-shaped when viewed from above. Surrounded by the hills of the Lower Galilee on the west, the Golan Heights on the east, and the Jordan Valley to the south, the lake's vistas seem all the more spectacular. Today, the lake supports a vigorous tourist industry and a rich agricultural economy, as well as the perennial fishing industry that has supported life around the lake from Jesus' time to the present.

In Jesus' time, the lake formed the boundary between the territories controlled by Herod's two sons, Philip and Antipas. Antipas controlled the west side of the lake, Philip the east. The north side of the lake was dominated by strictly observant Jews in the first century who chafed at Roman rule and seethed over the Herodians' collaboration with the pagan invaders.[2] From Tiberias southward, however, a different kind of Jew had settled on the west side of the lake, Jews more open to and inclusive of Gentiles, more assimilated to life under Roman occupation. Antipas, therefore, regarded the northern shore of the lake with great suspicion—a cauldron of revolution—and he watched the Jews there with a wary eye. The east side of the lake, controlled by Antipas's brother, Philip, was almost totally dominated by pagan settlers and nonobservant Jews who had no scruples about living in such close proximity to pagan peoples. Indeed, the east side of the lake was dominated by the Decapolis (from *deka,* meaning "ten," and *polis,* meaning "city"), a league of ten cities so thoroughly paganized and therefore not resistant to Roman (pagan) rule as was the Jewish population of Palestine, that the Romans did not even feel it necessary to place them under military rule like the rest of Palestine, but instead permitted them a measure of independence and autonomy. Strict Jews would not set foot in the Decapolis and avoided the east side of the lake whenever possible.

In this regard, it is significant that Jesus made Capernaum the center of his early ministry in Galilee. Situated on the north side of the lake, Capernaum was right in the middle of observant Jewish influence, yet only a short distance (less than a mile) from the territory of Philip and the paganism that dominated the eastern side of the lake. Capernaum had a customs office—situated as it was on the Via Maris (a Roman mile marker discovered during excavations at Capernaum confirms the town's presence on the Via Maris), the major road from Egypt in the south to Damascus and points north and east—so that persons traveling from the territory of Antipas to the territory of Philip had to stop and pay a toll to cross over. Matthew, Jesus' disciple, manned that tollbooth.

Matthew's Gospel has an interesting though nondescript passage that may speak to the political situation around the north end of the lake in Jesus' time. Matthew 4:12–13 says, "And having heard that John had been arrested, Jesus departed for the Galilee, and leaving Nazareth, he came and took up residence in Capernaum by the sea, in the regions of Zebulon and Nephtali." The text is interesting in that Jesus, upon learning that John the Baptist has just been arrested by Antipas (probably for conspiring to foment sedition by his radical, revolutionary preaching about the coming of the kingdom of God), and fearing that he would no doubt be next on Antipas's "hit list," leaves Nazareth (which Antipas controls) and moves to Capernaum (still in Antipas's territory, but only a short walk to the territory controlled by Philip, where Antipas cannot touch him). There among the observant Jews looking for the coming of God's kingdom, Jesus begins his preaching ministry, a ministry that, according to the

Gospels, is confined exclusively to the north end of the lake (from Magdala on the west to Gergesa on the east).

But in Mark's Gospel, Jesus frequently moves from west to east, traveling across the lake by boat (note Mark 5:1: "And he went to the other side of the sea, to the country of the Gerasenes"). For Jesus, to move from the west side of the lake to the east side was to move in more ways than one. He was moving not only geographically (west to east), but also politically (from Antipas's territory to Philip's), ethnically (from the Jewish world to the Gentile world), and religiously (from the world of Judaism to the world of paganism). Jesus, having identified himself as one of Israel's faithful by settling in Capernaum, was nonetheless provocative in his willingness to move among those whom Israel regarded as "godless" and "pagan." And so it was that on one of those journeys across the lake this happened. . . .

The Scripture: Mark 4:35–41

And [Jesus] said to them on that day, when evening had come, "Let us cross over to the other side." And having left the crowd, they took him [with them] as he was in the boat. But there were also other boats with him. And a great squall of wind arose, and the waves lashed at the boat so that already the boat was being filled [with water]. And he was in the stern, on a cushion, asleep. And [the disciples] were [attempting to] wake him and [were] saying to him, "Teacher, does it not matter to you that we are perishing?" And having awakened, he rebuked the wind and said to the sea, "Shut up! Be quiet!" And the wind stopped and there was a great calm. And he said to them, "Why are you afraid? Do you still have no faith?" And they feared a great fear, and they were saying to one another, "Who is this one that even the wind and the sea obey him?"

"Epiphany Stories"

Every time I go to Israel, people tell me "epiphany stories." Every time. So far as I know, I do nothing to elicit them. Typically, they happen on the bus, at the breakfast table, on a shopping excursion, or on a bathroom break. This rarely happens anywhere else. Just here. It must be the Land. Something about being in this place where so long ago God's presence, once thought to be distant, aloof, and transcendent, "broke out" and "broke through" and "broke in" to time and space and place, and thereby made all the difference in the world for somebody and delivered them from the encroaching chaos that threatened to overwhelm and engulf and subdue them—something about this place calls up from deep within us our own epiphany stories. The Land conjures in us those moments when, like the disciples of another time and another day, we too were confronted with an epiphany of God's presence—tactile, palpable, corporeal—and for us as for them, not a moment too soon, not a moment too late. On a recent trip to the Holy Land one overwhelmed pilgrim, in the presence of these constantly chronicled epiphany stories, just kept on repeating over and over again, like some sort of sacred mantra, "Well it is a land of miracles, you know."

It certainly was for those first disciples. Mark pictures them stupefied and dumbfounded in the face of the constant barrage of bewildering wonders that they had witnessed at the hands of Jesus. On more than one occasion they responded with chaotic confusion or muddled mystery to some miraculous feat performed by Jesus. "Who is this man that even the wind and the waves obey him?" they wanted to know.[3]

When the disciples spoke those words, the chaos was close at hand. Mark, for whom Jesus is preeminently the exorcist come to cast Satan and his minions out of the world so that he might reestablish God's sovereign rule, pictures Jesus, like some mad King Lear, screaming at the bedeviling wind and waves that threatened to swamp the boat. The language Jesus employed when he screamed at the wind is exactly the same language he had used in the synagogue at Capernaum when he exorcised the demon from the possessed man (Mark 1:21–28; see chapter 6). You see, in the ancient world the sea was thought to be possessed by demons who convulsed the water much as they do humans who are possessed. And so, much like possessed people, the possessed sea thrashed and foamed with demonic fury, driving wind and wave and water. It is for this reason that the sea had come to be associated in ancient times with the chaos monster. Most ancient Near Eastern cultures had creation stories that involved the subduing of the monster of chaos as a prelude to creation, and for many of those cultures the quintessential abode of chaos was the foaming, frothing, fulminating sea (Genesis 1:2: "And the earth was chaotic, without form, void, and darkness hovered over the face of the deep [*tehom*]"). It is probably in allusion to this imagery that John, in the book of Revelation, pictures the final culmination of the new creation with the words "and the sea was no more" (Revelation 21:1).

And so Mark pictures Jesus, Lord of Creation, in an epiphany of God's sovereign lordship (what Mark calls "the kingdom of God), banishing the chaos monster from the sea and bringing to the kingdom creation and calm. The bleary-eyed, disbelieving disciples are left scratching their heads in a "land of miracles" and muttering to themselves, "Who is this man that even the wind and the waves obey him?" Those first disciples must have gotten a good laugh out of that question when years later, reflecting on the fact that the Lord of the Universe was in the boat with them and yet they quivered and cowered in the face of chaos only to have him subdue the wind and calm the waves, they told on themselves this . . . this . . . epiphany story.

And two thousand years later another group of disciples gathers at the breakfast table and tells on themselves their own epiphany stories, those moments when the winds howled and the waves foamed and the chaos threatened, and they were rescued, not a moment too soon or a moment too late, by a breakthrough, an epiphany, of God's grace.

I have an epiphany story. Want to hear it?

My wife and I married while I was still in college. Financially it was tough. We both worked while I was finishing my undergraduate education. We had made a pact that we would not incur any indebtedness for college, knowing that the prospects of repaying a large educational loan were not good for one entering the ministry. I had already dropped out of school one semester in order to work full-time to save the money to reenter school the following year. But when I was facing my final semester in school, we calculated that we would be about $250 short of the tuition money needed for me to matriculate for my final semester. We had worked and saved and figured, and yet the money just wasn't there. Finally, after exhausting every apparent avenue, I decided that I would again drop out of school and work until I had made enough money to return and finish my degree. Of course, it would delay my entering seminary and completing my ministerial preparation, but there seemed to be no alternative. It was a painful decision, but one we felt we had no choice but to make.

The morning of registration a letter came in the mail from someone whose name I didn't recall. It was from a member of a Baptist church where I had spoken some months earlier. Inside was a check! The sender wrote, "I hope you won't be offended, but I just couldn't get you off my mind. I'm not sure why; you spoke here in our church months ago. But I felt I had to write you and send you this check to help you with your studies for the ministry. I don't know if you need the money, and I'm not sure whether or not this check will help in any way, but I felt compelled to send it to you as a small investment in your ministry."

Do you want to guess the amount of the check?

And hearing the winds cease and seeing the waves calmed, the bleary-eyed, disbelieving disciples looked at each other and asked, "Who is this man that even the wind and the waves obey him?"

But you know who he is. Don't you.

For Further Discussion

1. In light of recent archaeological discoveries at Sepphoris, Herod Antipas's capital just four miles northwest of Nazareth, how provincial and rural was Jesus' environment during his adolescence?
2. Why did Jesus make Capernaum the center of his operations during his Galilean ministry?
3. What was the significance of Jesus' frequent lake crossings?
4. How was Jesus' calming of the storm an exorcism? How was it an epiphany?
5. Have you had any epiphanies of God's grace in your life?

NOTES

1. *Biblical Archaeological Review* devoted a recent issue (July/August 2000) to the findings of more than fifteen years of digging at Sepphoris. The debate over the ethnic makeup of the city has important implications for our understanding of Jesus. Was he, as

some scholars suggest, a predominantly Jewish figure: either a first-century Jewish rabbi, on the one hand, or a Jewish reformer steeped in the classical Hebrew prophetic tradition, on the other? Or, as other scholars suggest, was he more like a peripatetic Greco-Roman philosopher, more at home in the world of Greco-Roman Hellenism than the world of first-century Judaism? The presence of Sepphoris so close to Nazareth means that Jesus was most assuredly more urbane than previously thought. But whether his perspectives were more influenced by Greco-Roman Hellenism or first-century Judaism is, in part, determined by the ethnic character of the major city in his immediate environment, namely, Sepphoris. Eric Meyers and Mark Chancey have argued, on the basis of their archaeological findings, that Sepphoris was a predominantly Jewish city, with Hellenistic influences, to be sure. The paucity of pig bones at the site (Jews, of course, would not eat pork), the presence of the fragmentary remains of stone vessels (Jews preferred stone vessels to pottery because the former were immune to ritual impurity), and the presence of Jewish ritual baths *(mikvaoth)* attest to a significant Jewish population in Sepphoris at the time of Jesus. See Mark Chancey and Eric Meyers, "How Jewish Was Sepphoris in Jesus' Time?" *Biblical Archaeological Review* 26, no. 4 (2000): 18–33, 61.

2. Herodians was the name given to the supporters of the Herodian dynasty in first-century Palestine. Herod and his sons were unpopular among observant Jews, as Herod the Great was not a Jew, but Idumean. Moreover, observant Jews disliked Herod's capitulation to and collaboration with the occupying Roman military presence.

3. Mark employs the language of fear and amazement to highlight the disciples' lack of understanding. See R. Wayne Stacy, "Fear in the Gospel of Mark" (Ph.D. diss., Southern Baptist Theological Seminary, 1979).

CHAPTER 4

Tabgha: Peter's Harbor

Located on the Via Maris (Way of the Sea), which turns east at Gennesaret and runs along the north end of the lake, about eight miles north of Tiberias and about a mile and a half west of Capernaum, is a lush, green oasis of a place called in Greek *Heptapegon*, the "seven springs," and in Arabic *Tabgha*, which is probably the Arabic corruption of the Greek. Aptly named for the artesian sulfur springs that bubble up to the surface at the site, Tabgha's waters green the surrounding landscape and empty their steady streams of warm, mineral-laden liquid into the lake at a natural hollow today called the Harbor of Peter. Especially in the winter and early spring, when the lake's water can become quite cold, large shoals of fish gather at Tabgha's harbor to rejuvenate themselves in the warm mineral bath of the seven springs, making the harbor a favorite spot for local fishers. In Jesus' day, Tabgha's harbor, just a short walk from Capernaum, was often crowded with fishing boats from Capernaum hauling in the harvest of herring and other small fish that gathered where the springs emptied into the lake. Even today, if you go to Tabgha early in the morning, you will find dozens of local fishers plying the warm waters for their favorite fish of the more than forty species that populate the lake—especially the so-called St. Peter's fish, the *musht,* a tropical transplant that suffers in the chilly winter waters of the lake and is therefore drawn like a magnet to Tabgha's tepid springs.[1]

It was just such a scene that John describes in his Gospel following the crucifixion of Jesus, when Simon Peter, along with several others of Jesus' disciples, had returned home to Capernaum frightened, frustrated, disillusioned, and defeated, there to take up again the trade that had sustained him in the time before he had been called by the Nazarene to become a "fisher of people." The pathos of the scene was particularly poignant for Simon because he had sworn allegiance to Jesus irrespective of cost or consequence. And yet, when the test came, Simon succumbed to self-interest and denied ever having known Jesus. And when Jesus died on that hot, hateful afternoon, he died abandoned by all, even by his trusted colleagues, even by his best friend, Simon. Years later, Mark would add the commentary to that awful anguish, and some believe that it was Simon who, out of his own personal purgatory, supplied the words "And we [disciples] all abandoned him and ran for our lives, every last one of us" (Mark 14:50). So, full of doubt and self-recrimination, Simon sought to assuage his guilt by returning to the friendly nets and familiar waters in which so often before he had spent far more productive nights than the ones he had just endured up in Jerusalem.

But this time, Tabgha taunted him. All night he fished without success. It seemed that having failed at being a "fisher of people," Simon would not be able even to return to being a fisher of fish.

But at daybreak, Simon and his fishing partners saw a stranger standing on the beach. The stranger called to them, "Did you guys have any luck last night?"

"Nah, not a thing."

"Well, why don't you try the other side of the boat?"

And Simon, no doubt, thought to himself, "I've been fishing these waters all my life, and this clown's gonna tell me how to fish?"

But out of frustration, or desperation, or just to shut this guy up, Simon threw the net into the water on the other side of the boat, and the catch of fish almost swamped them. John writes, "The disciple whom Jesus loved said, 'It's the Lord!'" And Simon swallowed hard, because about the last person he ever expected to see again was Jesus.

When they got to shore, there was Jesus, with a charcoal fire going and bread and fish for breakfast.[2] "Are you guys hungry?" he asked. But no one dared say a word. And Jesus broke bread and fried fish and fed them . . . again.

Finally, after what seemed an eternity, Jesus said to Simon, "Simon, son of John, do you love me more than these?" Jesus meant the nets, of course. It was painfully apparent to all that although Simon had professed his love for Jesus even to the point of dying for him, in point of fact, he didn't love him more than his nets. Simon managed to mutter, "Uh, sure Lord. You know I love you." And Jesus responded, "Then feed my lambs." Three times, once for each of Simon's denials, Jesus repeated the question, and three times Simon professed his love, a love that he and Jesus both knew was not what either of them had hoped it would be. And then, incredibly, the last thing Jesus ever said to Simon was the very first thing Jesus said to Simon: "Follow me."

To tell you the truth, my heart goes out to Simon. I know how he feels. Is there anything more painful than when the richness of life's promise collides with the poverty of life's achievement, and the smoke clears, and the dust settles, and we discover that we've betrayed our best friend?

Tabgha's story is a "Simon story." It's a story of failure and of forgiveness and of a future on the far side of failure. It's the story of Simon, son of John, and it's the story of Simon, son of Bill or Frank or Charles or James or Robert. It's his story; it's my story; it's your story. It's the story of promises made and promises broken. It's the story of a love that will never let us go and will never let us *off.*

It is at Tabgha, on the far side of failure, that the Savior meets us and beckons us once again, "Follow me."

The Scripture: John 21:1–19

After these things, Jesus manifested himself again to the disciples by the Sea of Tiberias. He manifested [himself] in this way.

Simon Peter and Thomas, the one called Twin, and Nathaniel, the one from Cana of Galilee, and the sons of Zebedee, and two others of his disciples were together. Simon Peter said to them, "I am going fishing." They said to him, "We're going too." They went out and embarked on the boat, but that night they caught nothing.

Just as it was becoming morning, Jesus stood on the shore, but the disciples did not know that it was Jesus. Jesus said to them, "Children, have you got anything to eat?" They answered him, "No." He said to them, "Then cast your net on the right side of the boat, and you will find [some]." So they did, and they were not able to haul it in because there were so many fish [in it]. Then, that disciple whom Jesus loved said to Peter, "It is the Lord!" Then Simon Peter, having heard that it was the Lord, put on his clothes, for he was naked, and jumped into the lake. But the other disciples came in the boat, dragging the net of fish, for they were not far from land, only about a hundred yards away.

Then, when they reached land, they saw a charcoal fire burning, with fish and bread lying on it. Jesus said to them, "Bring some of the fish that you just caught." And so Simon Peter went and dragged the net ashore, full with about a hundred and fifty large fish; and though there were so many, the net was not torn. Jesus said to them, "Come and have breakfast." But none of the disciples dared ask him, "Who are you?" knowing that he was the Lord. And Jesus came and took the bread and gave [it] to them, and so also the fish. This was the third [time] Jesus was manifested to the disciples, having been raised from the dead.

When they had finished breakfast, Jesus said to Simon Peter, "Simon, son of John, do you love me more than these?" He said to him, "Yes, Lord, you know that I love

you." He said to him, "Feed my lambs." He said again to him a second [time], "Simon, son of John, do you love me?" He said to him, "Yes, Lord, you know that I love you." He said to him, "Feed my sheep." He said to him the third [time], "Simon, son of John, do you love me?" Peter was grieved that he said to him the third time, "Do you love me?" And he said to him, "Lord, you know all things; you know that I love you." Jesus said to him, "Feed my sheep. Amen, amen, I say to you, when you were young, you dressed yourself and walked about wherever you wished. But when you are old, you will reach out your hand, and another will dress you and carry you where you do not wish to go." This he said signifying by what sort of death he was to glorify God. And after this he said, "Follow me."

"A Simon Story"

My good friend Truett Gannon tells a "Simon story." Truett grew up in Cordele, Georgia, though he had not been back to Cordele for some time, his parents having moved away years earlier. Years later, Truett, who by then was already well established in ministry, was asked back to his hometown to preach a revival. While he was there, he decided to visit all his old haunts: the football stadium where he had played high school football; the malt shop where he had whiled away so many warm, lazy Georgia afternoons; the open field where, back in the 1940s, all the men in town had been loaded onto troop trains and shipped off to war. Truett stopped his car by that field, got out, and started remembering. He recalled a day, back when he was eleven years old, when on a Sunday afternoon everyone in that little south Georgia town had gone down to the train depot to watch the men being loaded onto troop trains to be sent off to fight in World War II. Everyone in town had someone on one of those troop trains, everyone except Truett. He went down to the depot because everyone else in town was there.

Amid tearful shouts of goodbye from anguished mothers and wives and girlfriends, Truett watched as the final car passed by. And there, standing in the doorway of the last car, was Sam Roobin, holding on to the railing. Sam was nineteen, the high school football star, and Truett's hero. And there he was going off to war with all the other men. And as the car pulled away, Sam waved to everyone and to no one. Then, picking little Truett out of the crowd, he looked straight at him, waved, and said, "Goodbye, Truett." Truett said that it just wasn't possible to describe how that made an eleven-year-old boy from a little South Georgia town feel, knowing that someone, going so far away to do such a big thing, would pick *him* out of the crowd and call *him* by name.

Standing in that field and recalling that moment, Truett realized that, though he had seen Sam on many occasions subsequent to that event when visiting his parents on trips to Cordele, he had never told Sam how much that experience had meant to him through the years. And so he decided to visit Roobin's Department Store, which had been owned by Sam's father but which Sam now ran, to tell Sam how much he had appreciated what he had done and said that day all those years ago. He walked in and greeted Sam. And when Truett told him how much his goodbye had meant to him, Sam said, "Let me tell you what happened to me after I left Cordele."

"The army sent me to Cleveland, Ohio," Sam said, "for three days before basic training. I knew no one in Cleveland, but I liked to play golf, so I looked up the number of a country club in Cleveland and called to see if I could play. They said to come on down, and so I did. They fixed me up with clubs and shoes, and while I was tying my shoes, the club pro said, 'Here's a threesome that needs a partner. If you're willing to tee off with them, you can play now.' I said, 'Okay,' and so the other three began to introduce themselves to me. When I told them my name, one of them said, 'Son, are you from south Georgia?' I said, 'Yes, sir.' He said, 'Does your father run a department store in Cordele?' I said, 'Yes, sir, he does.' And with that, the man literally fell on me and embraced me. Then he said, 'Sam, I owe my life to your father.' Then he told me his story. He said, 'I was a traveling salesman who had been down on my luck and who drank heavily. I was arrested and thrown in jail one night while traveling through Cordele. But while I was there, a man came to the jail, bailed me out, took me home with him, let me get a bath, and set a place for me at his table that night for supper. It was the first good meal I'd eaten in weeks. After supper, he took me to his store, gave me a new suit of clothes, and then he said to me, "I don't know what brought you to this place or how you got here, but in the name of God, I pray that you never make this kind of mistake again." That was years ago. With God's help, I've turned my life around. I'm sober, married with a beautiful family, and the district supervisor of my company. That man, Sam, was your father!'"

Now, what are the chances that a man who had affected Truett's life in such a wonderful and marvelous way would, some twenty years after the fact, tell him a "Simon story" about going to Cleveland, Ohio, running his finger through the Yellow Pages, and picking out the one country club where he would play golf in the one foursome in which he would meet the one man who years earlier had been forgiven and redeemed by his father? What are the chances of that happening? About as much as running into a dead man down by the lake.

I tell you the truth—that can only happen in Christ! But in Christ, it can happen.

For Further Discussion

1. Why was (and is) the fishing so good at Tabgha?
2. Why did Simon Peter return to Capernaum and his former occupation of fishing following Jesus' crucifixion?
3. To what was Jesus referring when he asked Simon, "Do you love me more than these?"
4. Why was Simon grieved that Jesus asked him three times, "Do you love me more than these?"
5. Do you have a "Simon story" to tell?

NOTES

1. Perhaps the leading expert on life around the Sea of Galilee is the eighty-two-year-old Mendel Nun, whom I met years ago while leading a study tour in Israel. Nun, though not a professional archaeologist, frequently contributes to archaeological journals regarding the Galilee environs. See, for example, Mendel Nun, "Cast Your Net upon the Waters: Fish and Fishermen in Jesus' Time," *Biblical Archaeological Review* 19, no. 6 (1993): 46–56, 70; "Ports of Galilee," *Biblical Archaeological Review* 25, no. 4 (1999): 18–31, 64.

2. The Greek word translated "charcoal fire," *anthrakia,* occurs only twice in the New Testament, here at John 21:9, and at John 18:18, where Simon, having just denied his Lord, warms himself by a charcoal fire!

CHAPTER 5

The Mount of the Beatitudes

On the northwestern shore of the lake known in the Bible as the Sea of Galilee is a region, triangular in shape, that was anchored by three cities in Jesus' time: Capernaum, Korazin, and Bethsaida. It is known today among biblical scholars and archaeologists as the "Evangelical Triangle."[1] The westernmost point of the triangle was delineated by the village of Tabgha, the northernmost by Korazin, and the easternmost by Bethsaida, with Capernaum situated in the center of the triangle's base. Just to the west of Capernaum rises a ridge of hills, the highest of which is known as the "mountain of Capernaum." This mountain is almost certainly the one referred to by Matthew when he says that, following the resurrection, the eleven disciples returned to Galilee to the "mountain to which Jesus had directed them" (Matthew 28:16). Because the mountain is rock-strewn and craggy, it was not suitable for cultivation and therefore was left isolated and relatively untouched by the local farmers and villagers. It was probably to this isolated, unspoiled hillside that Jesus retreated to pray when the press of the crowds who pursued him proved too much for his spirit. Mark no doubt refers to this hillside when he reports that "early in the morning, before the sun arose, [Jesus] went out to a lonely place [*erēmos topos*] and there he prayed" (Mark 1:35). But the crowds pursued him nonetheless. And so, according to Matthew, Jesus gathered them together on that "mount" and delivered to them his "sermon" on the nature of life in the kingdom of God, the so-called Sermon on the Mount. Early Christian pilgrims to the Holy Land were so convinced that this hillside was the place where Jesus preached the Sermon that they named it "Eremos," the "lonely place" referred to in Mark 1:35.

A Christian Spanish pilgrim of the fourth century named Egeria chronicled her visit to Capernaum and Tabgha. When she asked the locals to take her to the place where Jesus preached the Sermon, she says that they took her to a grotto in a hillside near Tabgha, the place of the seven springs. Just above the grotto, on the precipice of the hillside, is a terrace known as Mughara Ayub. From that vantage point one can overlook the entire lake and the surrounding villages. Moreover, the terrace provides a natural speaking platform from which, with a minimum of projection, the speaker may be heard by a large crowd gathered below. It was this hill, she was told, upon which the Lord ascended when he taught the Beatitudes.[2]

In the fourth century, a church was erected near the site where Jesus preached the Sermon. Egeria refers to this church when she says, "Past the walls of this church goes the public highway [Via Maris] on which the Apostle Matthew had his place of custom. Near there on a mountain is the cave to which the Saviour climbed and spoke the Beatitudes."[3] Though the church was destroyed in the seventh century, its ruins and the cave itself can still be seen above the Roman road.

To replace the church, the Franciscans enlisted Italian architect Antonio Barluzzi to design a chapel further up the Eremos. The chapel, built in 1938, now commemorates the site on which the Lord delivered the Sermon on the Mount. The octagonal-shaped church (eight-sided to commemorate the eight Beatitudes and that the number eight was an early Christian symbol for resurrection) features beautiful stained-glass depictions of each Beatitude. Surrounded by manicured grounds, lush gardens, and beautiful vistas of the lake, the chapel offers a tranquil setting from which to contemplate the meaning of Jesus' declarations about that quality he calls "blessed."

The Scripture: Matthew 5:1–10

And having seen the crowds, he ascended onto a mountain, and when he had sat down, his disciples came to him. And having opened his mouth, he taught them, saying,

> **"Blessed are the poor in spirit, for theirs is the kingdom of heaven.**
> **Blessed are they who mourn, for they shall be comforted.**
> **Blessed are the meek, for they shall inherit the earth.**
> **Blessed are they who hunger and thirst for righteousness, for they shall be satisfied.**
> **Blessed are they who are merciful, for they shall receive mercy.**
> **Blessed are the pure in heart, for they shall see God.**
> **Blessed are the peacemakers, for they shall be called children of God.**
> **Blessed are they who have been persecuted for the sake of righteousness, for theirs is the kingdom of heaven."**

"The Measure of Our Success"

Several years ago, when my wife, Cheryl, and I moved to Raleigh, we secured a copy of the dreaded North Carolina Driver's License Examination Booklet and began to study for the driver's exam, otherwise known as "state-sanctioned humiliation therapy." We went on the same day to take the exam. We both passed. But I had no more than gotten seated in the car and buckled my seat belt when she started: "I missed only one; how many did you miss?"

"Two. I missed two. There, are you happy now?"

Life is a test, and it's very important in this test called life that we be able to tell the winners from the losers. What? No one ever told you that?

Buy a new home or car. You think you're filling out a credit application? Wrong. You're taking a test. Bet you didn't know that there were *right* answers to those questions, did you?

Have you noticed that when you go to the doctor's office for a checkup, the first thing they do is weigh you? Well, that should be no big deal; I step on the scales every morning of my life. I think I can handle it all by myself. But notice: the nurse never says, "Now, just go over there to the scales and weigh yourself and then come back and tell me what it said." Oh no. The nurse stands there, looking over your shoulder, reading it too. It's a test.

But there's no evaluation that strikes terror in the hearts of most of us more than the dreaded invitation to our twenty-fifth high school reunion. You didn't know that this is a test? How naive. Weight Watchers would go out of business without high school reunions.

Months before you get there you start asking yourself, "I wonder whatever became of old so-and-so?" Of course, what you really mean is, "I wonder who in our class turned out to be 'winners' and who turned out to be 'losers'?" And we know how to tell, don't we? Who married the best-looking kid in the class or who married the star athlete? Who will drive up in the Lexus and who will drive up in the old, beat-up Plymouth Duster?

It's a test. Sure it is. We measure the winners and losers in "how muches" and "how manys." How much weight have you gained? How much money do you make? How many times have you been divorced?

Life is a test, and in any test it is important to be able to tell the "winners" from the "losers." That's why we have those special classes for the "talented and gifted." You know what I mean. Why don't we just go ahead and call the rest the "untalented and ungifted"? Or why don't we just go ahead and call them what we really mean: winners and losers?

And who decides anyway? I guess that on the first day of school each year, the principal divides you up into two groups: "All right now, all you 'talented and gifted' people over here. The rest of you over there."

See how it feels! And note: by the typical definition of "talented and gifted," people such as Thomas Edison and Steven Hawkings would have been characterized as losers.

Now don't misunderstand me. I'm not denying that in the game called life there are winners and losers. The stakes are higher than we think. I'm only pointing out that the moment we speak of "winners and losers," two related questions arise: Who decides? And by what criteria?

When you go to your class reunion, how will you tell the "winners" from the "losers"? How do you evaluate it? How do you take the measure of success? The values we employ in evaluating "winners and losers" say at least as much about us as they do about the persons we thus evaluate.

I wonder. Had you been on the mountainside with Jesus that afternoon when the crowd of cripples and diseased and incorrigible came staggering up to hear him, and he looked out over that group of "losers" and then turned to his disciples and said, "Blessed are the poor in spirit, for the kingdom of heaven belongs to them," would you have bought it? Or would you have been roaming the parking lot looking for the Lexuses and BMWs?

That's what he's saying, you know. "Blessed," *makarios* in Greek, *baruch* in Hebrew, was a common literary locution in the Old Testament and Judaism. Owing to the Hebrew idea that words are a form of power with a vitality and energy all their own quite apart from the speaker, to bless someone was not merely to say something to them or even about them, but to *do* something for them and to them.

I'll never forget the first time this performative quality of the Hebrew concept of "blessing" came home to me. It was in my beginner's Sunday school class, and we were studying how Jacob tricked his father, Isaac, out of the paternal blessing that rightfully belonged to his older brother, Esau. You remember the story. Jacob came in to see his old, sick, half-blind father and was wearing animal skins on his arms to mimic his brother Esau's hirsute appearance. Isaac felt Jacob's arms, and thinking he was talking to Esau, his firstborn, he pronounced the paternal blessing on the wrong kid. How embarrassing!

When I first heard that story, I remember thinking, "What's the deal? Why didn't he just take it back? Why didn't he just do what we used to call a 'do-over'?" You know, when I was little and did something that didn't turn out right, I just declared a do-over—that's what we called it, kind of like a mulligan in golf. "Uh oh! Blessed the wrong kid! I take it back!" I still remember asking my Sunday school teacher why Isaac couldn't just "take it back." She said little kids weren't supposed to ask questions like that. But think about it. Why not? I'll tell you why. Because the blessing, once spoken, like an arrow flung from a bow, took on a life of its own and was irretrievable. Esau knew. Who will ever forget his anguished cry when he looks at his old, dying father, Isaac, and asks, "Do you have only one blessing, my father? Bless me, even me also, O my father!"

Which makes all the more incredible what Jesus says in the Sermon: "Blessed are the poor in spirit . . . blessed are they who mourn . . . blessed are the meek . . . blessed are the persecuted." But these are not the people whom we would ordinarily regard as "blessed" in any meaningful sense. These are not the folk we'd put in the "talented and gifted" group. I mean, these are the people who drove to the class reunion in the old, beat-up Plymouth Duster, for heaven's sake. And yet, Jesus calls them "blessed."

And the congregation, then and now, does a double take. "What? The diseased, the poor, the dysfunctional—blessed? In the kingdoms of this world, if you are unemployed, people treat you like a pariah. In the kingdoms of this world, the terminally ill are regarded as a drain on the health care system. Give me a break. How can these people be blessed?"

And Jesus says, "Oh, I'm sorry. My mistake. I should have been clearer. I'm not talking about the way things are in the world's kingdoms. I'm talking about the kingdom of God. You see, in God's kingdom there's a very, very different way to take the measure of our success. In the kingdom of God, it's not about who you are or what you can do or what you have. Matter of fact, it's not about you at all. It's about God. In God's kingdom, God determines the value of things, and because God values everything, everything has value. You see, God doesn't love you because you're valuable; you're valuable because God loves you. It's the way of things in God's kingdom. And so don't be fooled by appearances. You can't tell the 'winners' from the 'losers' until you know the name of the game."

I have a friend in West Virginia whom I have known since college. I may be the minister, but if ever I've known a Christian, it is he. He is one of the most generous, unassuming, gracious, meek, God-fearing persons I know.

Life has not always been easy for him. School was difficult, though he was far from lazy; indeed, he worked harder than most of us in school, and getting good marks was always a struggle for him. He closed the library every night in school, and yet a C was about the best grade he could ever manage. I remember that his advisor once told him that he probably should consider transferring to a vocational-technical school—just not "college material," he said in an attempt at diplomacy.

But my friend had a vision. He wanted to teach in the public school system and to coach athletics to disadvantaged boys, boys who, without anyone at home to teach them or to pass on to them the legacy of how to measure real success, might have ended up in jail or in prison or worse. All he ever wanted to do was make a difference, to give something back. It wasn't that he was trying to be a saint or a martyr; it was more what Marian Wright Edelman said in her book *The Measure of Our Success:* "Service to others is the rent we pay for living in this world."[4]

Well, finally he finished school and began his coaching career in basketball at a middle school in his home state of West Virginia. He believed that this was the right age to try to make a difference in these boys' lives—seventh, eighth, and ninth graders. Well, it was tough. He didn't make much money, and the work was frustrating. These kids came from homes where the parents didn't know where they were or what they were doing and didn't much care. Most were on drugs by the time they were in the fifth grade. Night after night he would be called down to the police station. One of the boys would get in trouble and the police wouldn't be able to locate a parent or relative, so they'd call my friend. He'd go down there, sign the boy out, and take him home—such as it was. Not much of a job, if prestige is what you're about. But he wasn't working for money or power; he was working for something some people will never understand.

Slowly, imperceptibly at first, the kids began to understand that this man really cared; that he was not just "passing through on his way up," but really wanted to help. And so they started to trust him. The team got better, too. Several of the boys went on to high school and even to college on athletic scholarships. None of them ever forgot my friend.

Budget cuts in public school education forced the state to defund middle school athletics, and so my friend's program was terminated. But when the local newspaper wanted to do a story on him, the boys had to stand in line to be interviewed.

My wife and I spent some time with him and his wife this summer in the mountains of western North Carolina. We talked about a lot of things, both of us having reached midlife. He told me about his experience of going to his twenty-fifth high school reunion some years earlier. He talked about how "successful" some of his classmates had become—a physician, several attorneys, some "successful" businessmen. There was no trace of envy in his voice, maybe even a little pride that his friends had done so well. That's just who he is.

With only the sound of crickets chirping to break the silence between us, my friend looked at me and said, "You know something, Wayne, I know this may sound crazy, but I wouldn't have traded places with anyone in that room."

"Yeah," I said. "Some might say that's crazy. I have another name for it. You know what I'd call it? I'd call it 'blessed.' That's what I'd call it—blessed."

For Further Discussion

1. What was the "Evangelical Triangle"?

2. Why did Jesus preach his Sermon on the Mount from atop the rocky escarpment known, in Mark's Gospel, as *erēmos topos,* "lonely place"?

3. What was the subject of Jesus' Sermon on the Mount?

4. What was the significance of Jesus' use of the word "blessed"?

5. Do you ever feel as though you're "playing a different game" than everyone else?

NOTES

1. Bargil Pixner, *With Jesus through Galilee* (Rosh Pina, Israel: Corazin Publishing, 1992), 34.

2. Ibid., 36–40.

3. Jerome Murphy-O'Connor, *The Holy Land: An Archaeological Guide from Earliest Times to 1700,* rev. ed. (New York: Oxford University Press), 233.

4. Marian Wright Edelman, *The Measure of Our Success: A Letter to My Children and Yours* (Boston: Beacon Press, 1992), 6.

CHAPTER 6

Capernaum

Situated on the Via Maris about a mile and a half west of the Seven Springs (Tabgha), only a hundred yards or so from Lake Genessaret, is a site variously known as Tell Hum, Kefr Nahum, and Capernaum. The three names almost certainly refer to the same place. *Kefr Nahum* is Hebrew for "village of Nahum," whether of the biblical Nahum or not is uncertain. Capernaum *(Kapharnaoum)* is the Greek equivalent of Kefr Nahum. In time, as the village was destroyed and deserted, *kefr* was changed to *tell*, referring to an artificial hill preserving the ruins of a deserted city, and *Nahum* was shortened to *hum;* hence, Kefr Nahum (Capernaum) became Tell Hum.

In Jesus' day, anyone wishing to travel from Damascus in the north to Egypt in the south would have had to pass through this ancient fishing village. From Damascus, one would have crossed the Jordan at Bethsaida (et-Tell) just northeast of Capernaum where, in the first century though not today, the Jordan emptied into the lake. Then, one would have proceeded westward through Capernaum (Kefr Nahum), Tabgha, the Plain of Gennesaret, Magdala, the Valley of the Wind (Wadi el-Hamam), the Plain of Jezreel (Esdraelon), past Megiddo to the coast of the Mediterranean and on down to Egypt.

Excavations of Tell Hum (Capernaum) began under the direction of Charles Wilson in 1865. Then, at the end of the nineteenth century, the site came under the control of the Franciscans, who have excavated at Capernaum for a century. In attempting to ascertain the significance of Capernaum for recovering the Galilean ministry of Jesus, primary attention was given by Franciscan archaeologist Gaudence Orfali to the ruins of an ancient synagogue at the site. Excavations done in 1953 and 1954 revealed that beneath the ruins of the visible synagogue, considered by scholars to date to the fourth century, were foundation stones considerably older, perhaps even first century. That the stones of the older structure were of black basalt (volcanic rock indigenous to the area), whereas the stones of the newer structure were of white limestone (not indigenous to the area), gave credence to the Franciscans' view that the newer, fourth-century synagogue was erected on the ruins of the earlier, first-century synagogue. If so, it is likely that this older, first-century synagogue was the very synagogue in which Jesus preached when he lived in Capernaum at the home of Simon Peter (see Mark 1:21–34).[1]

More recently, however, the attention of archaeologists has been drawn southward of the synagogue to the remains of an octagonal-shaped building first revealed by Orfali in 1921, and excavated by Italian archaeologist Virgilio Corbo in 1968. Octagonal imagery was very important to the early church in that the number eight represented the eighth day, that is, resurrection day (Sunday, one day more than Saturday, the Sabbath, which Jews regarded as the seventh day), the day Jesus arose from the dead. Consequently, eight-sided architecture held tremendous significance for early Christians, many of them constructing their churches and baptisteries in the form of an octagon.[2] Moreover, it was the practice of the earliest Christian community to construct churches, typically eight-sided, over sites where significant events in the life of Christ were thought to have occurred, as a type of monument commemorating those events.

Additionally, literary evidence exists that as early as the fourth century, Christian pilgrims venerated the octagonal-shaped site as the place where Jesus resided while in Capernaum, namely, the house of Simon Peter.[3] In the record of her visit to Capernaum in 385, the Christian pilgrim Aetheria said of this site, "In Capernaum out of the house of the first of the apostles [Peter] a church was made, the walls of which stand until today as they once were."[4] One hundred and eighty-five years later, the anonymous Christian known as the Pilgrim of Piacenza wrote of the site, "We came to

Capernaum into the house of St. Peter, which is a basilica."[5] The Pilgrim's comments may suggest that the earlier church, reported by Aetheria, had been enlarged into a basilica. Indeed, this view seems to comport with the archaeology of the site. In the excavations done by Corbo in the 1920s and subsequent excavations in the 1980s by the Benedictine Bargil Pixner, the mystery of the Capernaum octagon began to emerge. It appears that a Byzantine basilica had been constructed on top of an earlier house church, which, in turn, had been constructed on top of (and out of) a first-century fisherman's quarters. Some of the rooms in the earlier fisherman's house had been adapted, by means of ornamentation and graffiti, for Christian worship, perhaps as early as the second century. In any case, it appears that this fisherman's house was used by early Christians as a house of worship from the second through the fourth centuries, whereupon it was converted into an octagonal-shaped Christian church.[6]

The evidence is fairly compelling that this octagonal-shaped site in Capernaum is actually the house of Simon Peter, and the place Jesus called home during his ministry in the Galilee.[7] On the strength of this archaeological evidence, the Franciscans, as did their Christian forebears, proceeded in the late 1980s to construct a church on the site. The Church of the House of St. Peter (Beata Petrus Domus), however, has been masterfully constructed so as not to obscure the archaeological excavations. The church is raised up on pylons above the site so that the excavations beneath can still be viewed, preserving the site and making it available to pilgrims at the same time.[8]

It is significant that Jesus chose Kefr Nahum, Capernaum, as his base of operations during his early ministry. Matthew, who is sensitive to such things, picks up on that significance when he states, "And [Jesus], having heard that John had been arrested, departed for Galilee. And leaving

Nazareth, he settled in Capernaum by the sea in the regions of Zebulon and Naphtali, in order that the word spoken by the prophet Isaiah might be fulfilled: 'The land of Zebulon and the land of Naphtali, the way of the sea, beyond the Jordan, Galilee of the Gentiles, a people dwelling in darkness have seen a great light, and among those dwelling in the region and shadow of death light has dawned'" (Matthew 4:12–16; cf. Isaiah 9:1–2).

Capernaum by the sea in Galilee of the Gentiles would be Jesus' base of operations during his early ministry. The significance of that description is made clearer when one considers that the Greek word translated "Gentiles" *(ethnē)* renders a Hebrew word *(goyim)* that, in both languages, also means "pagans." Galilee, unlike Judea, was populated by pagans, and by Jews whose scruples were not offended by living in close proximity to pagans. This situation is all the more remarkable when one remembers that Jews regarded themselves as the "chosen" of God and the rest of the teeming masses as "pagan," the primary metaphor for which was the foaming, formless, chaotic sea. Observant Jews, therefore, avoided contact with this "sea of paganism," as well as with Jews who associated with pagans, whenever possible. For Jesus to take up residence in "Capernaum by the sea" in "Galilee Goyim" meant that Jesus' early ministry occurred precisely among those whom observant Jews would have regarded as religiously suspect and whose beliefs and practices would have been considered abhorrent by pious Jews.

In this regard, then, it is not at all surprising that so much of Jesus' early ministry in and around the Galilee took the form of engagement with demons and evil spirits. Unlike Jews, whose belief in the oneness of God restrained the emergence of a developed demonology, pagan peoples believed that the world was filled with demons who menaced the population at every turn. The evidence from Megiddo, the Galilean hilltop fortress overlooking the Plain of Esdraelon, indicates that the indigenous Canaanite population of the region sacrificed pigs in an attempt to propitiate the demon spirits who threatened them (see Mark 5:1–20). And yet, Jesus, as the Isaianic prophecy declared, believed that part of his ministry was to be a "light to the Gentiles" in Capernaum by the sea in Galilee of the Gentiles (Isaiah 9:1–2; 42:6; 49:6). And so he engaged the demons and he "faced the forces" wherever he encountered them—in the graveyard at Gergesa, out on the foaming, frothing, storm-driven Galilean sea, or in the synagogue at Capernaum.

The Scripture: Mark 1:21–28

And they entered into Capernaum. And immediately on the sabbath, having entered into the synagogue, he began to teach. And they were astounded at his teaching, for he was teaching them as having authority and not as the scribes. And immediately a man with an unclean spirit was in their synagogue, and he cried out, saying, "What have you to do with us, Jesus the Nazarene? Have you come to destroy us? We know who you are—the Holy One of God." And Jesus rebuked him, saying, "Shut up and come out of him." And the unclean spirit, having convulsed him and having cried with a loud voice, came out of him. And all were amazed, so that they questioned one another, saying, "What is this? A new teaching? With authority he even commands the unclean spirits and they obey him." And his reputation went out immediately everywhere into the entire region of the Galilee.

"Facing the Forces"

As any good novelist or cinema director knows, the opening scene in which the central character is introduced to the audience is critical to the success of the story. It is in this scene that the audience gets its first glimpse of the hero, and as we all know, first impressions are important. The audience can "get a fix" on the hero: What kind of character is the hero? Is he dark and foreboding or comical? Will the audience be comfortable with the hero's moral values? Will they identify with her and her struggles? All this begins to take shape in that first scene in which the audience meets the hero.

And the Gospel writers are good storytellers. They pay special attention to the scene in which their central character, Jesus, is first seen engaging in activity that will be portrayed as typical of him in their respective Gospels. It is their way of "framing" Jesus for their audience, guiding the audience toward the interpretation of Jesus that is crucial to their individual portrayals of him. For example, in Matthew, the first glimpse we get of Jesus is as teacher. Jesus ascends the mountain and delivers his Sermon on the Mount to his disciples. And so for Matthew, Jesus is teacher. For Luke, Jesus is preacher. The first glimpse we get of Jesus in Luke is in the synagogue in Nazareth delivering his sermon to the hometown folk gathered for worship. For John, Jesus is most often healer giving grace, as to the cripple by the pool at Bethesda.

But here in Mark, Jesus is exorcist, casting the demons out of a man in the synagogue at Capernaum. For Mark, then, this is the lens through which he would have us view Jesus—Jesus the exorcist. "However else you understand Jesus," Marks says, "whether as teacher or preacher or healer, if you see him as I see him, you must see him as the one who opposes evil, the one who faces the forces." It is a consistent portrayal of Jesus throughout Mark's Gospel.

Most of the healings that Jesus performs in Mark's Gospel are really exorcisms. When Mark says that Jesus healed someone with an "unclean spirit," that's a euphemism for demon possession. The adjective "unclean" merely defines demon possession ritually rather than in terms of its force for harm.

And when Jesus calms the storm in Mark's Gospel, he's actually casting the demons out of the water. Don't be fooled by the translation "Peace! Be still!" That's not what the Greek says. The Greek says, *Siōpa, pephimōso,* "Shut up! Be silenced!" It's exorcism language, the same kind of language Jesus used in the synagogue at Capernaum when he cast the demon from the man with the unclean spirit: "Be silent! Come out of him!"

And so for Mark, if you want to understand who Jesus is, you must see him as the exorcist, the one who "faces the forces" and opposes evil wherever he encounters it—in the wilderness, at sea, or in the church. In Mark's Gospel, as in those of Matthew and Luke, Jesus is presented without apology as exorcising demons.

Interestingly, the Gospel of John has no exorcisms. You see, not everybody, then or now, believes in demons. It's just one of many ways of attempting to explain the gravity, the immensity of evil in the world.

Now, I don't mean the kind of evil that results from deliberate human choice—you know, the kind of evil we perpetrate on each other. Indeed, I think that "evil" is too big a word for that. A better word would be "meanness." To be sure, "meanness" participates in this cosmic, corporate evil, but it results primarily from human choice. We voluntarily choose to participate in this kind of evil. But that's not what I mean. I mean the kind of evil that lies beyond anybody's decision. Children are born twisted, crippled, blind, mute, epileptic. "Can you help him, Jesus? He throws himself into the water; he throws himself into the fire. His mother and I are afraid he's going to kill himself!" A hurricane strikes, a tornado hits, an earthquake levels a city, a raging fire consumes everything in sight, and the insurance people call it an "act of God." Do you see what they're doing? They're trying to describe this immense, impersonal, cosmic evil in the world that lies beyond anybody's choice. Frederick Buechner says, "To take the Devil seriously is to take seriously the fact that the total evil in the world is greater than the sum of all its parts."[9] What do you call it? How do you say it? Well, in Jesus' day some said it was the work of demons. "Yeah, the *demons* did it!"

And so, Mark presents the Savior of the world as one who opposes evil; he must if he's to save us in any meaningful sense. And in this characterization of Jesus as exorcist, Mark presents Jesus not only as opposing evil, but also as being able to discern evil's presence. Did you get it in the story? A man, full of demons, comes up to Jesus in the synagogue and says, "We know who you are! You're the Holy One of God!"

Now, that's not bad. Matter of fact, that's good. The demon calls him "the Holy One of God." That's a confession of faith, isn't it? It was true, wasn't it? But listen to Jesus: "Shut up, you demon, and come out of him!" Why did Jesus do that? Wasn't the demon right? Well, there's right, and then there's *right,* and it takes a lot of discernment to know the difference.

Jesus once said that there's a way that is right and there's a way that only seems right (Matthew 7:13–14), and the problem is that most of the time they look the same. Later on in Mark's story, at Caesarea Philippi, Jesus screams at someone, "Get behind me, Satan!"—and he was talking at the time to his best friend. It isn't always so simple to tell the difference between good and evil, is it?

Sometimes people do all the right things for all the wrong reasons and end up doing irreparable harm. And sometimes people who are roundly criticized and castigated for their conduct are, upon further reflection, doing the will of God. Is there anything more crucial than knowing what to affirm and what to oppose, what to bless and what to curse, what to stand for and what to stand against? It takes a lot of discernment, sometimes, to face the forces. And finally, only the spirit of Christ can dispatch them: "Shut up! Come out!" If we're going to face the forces—and face them we must—then perhaps we'd be wise and discerning to look around and make sure that whether we're standing for or standing against, we're standing with Jesus.

Dr. Ernest Campbell, retired pastor of Riverside Church in New York City, tells of an incident when he was serving a church in Ann Arbor, Michigan.[10] It seems that a few days after the assassination of President Kennedy, someone in Dr. Campbell's church brought to his attention the plight of Lee Harvey Oswald's widow, Marina. Because her husband had been accused of murdering the president, and through no fault of her own, she had become persona non grata. No one would have anything to do with her. Furthermore, because she was Russian and could speak very little English, she was quite alone and defenseless in this country. The suggestion was made that Marina Oswald could be brought to Ann Arbor to live under the auspices of the church while she learned to speak better English and acquired some means of gainful employment so as to be able to survive in this country. Dr. Campbell approved of the idea, and yet he recognized the potential for conflict over so daring a venture. And so, without bringing the matter to the attention of the entire congregation, lest it founder in a sea of suspicion, but with the consent of the executive committee in the church, Dr. Campbell got in touch with Marina Oswald.

In due time and with the cooperation of the FBI and others, Marina was brought to Ann Arbor to live. She slipped in under cover of night by train while a battery of reporters waited hawkishly at the airport. She lived with a modest family that took seriously its devotion to God and its love for people.

When finally the secret could be contained no longer, the church issued a brief press release. Immediately, the mail began to pour in. There were some who were quick and hot to say that what the church had done was unpatriotic. Others told Dr. Campbell that their action was unwise, and others that it was unfair. One woman said that she had belonged to a church for forty years and what it had done for her in all that time she could write on the back of a postage stamp! Others were prompted to say that what the church did was grossly un-American.

Dr. Campbell answered every letter and, in essence, told each one the same thing: You have suggested that we were unwise, or indiscreet, or un-American, or even just plain stupid. We may be, in fact, all of those things and a whole lot more. But the one thing you have not shown us is that what we have done is unlike Christ. Do that, do that, and you shall have our undivided attention.

When it comes time to face the forces, to take a stand, one will need all the discernment one can manage. But even that may not be enough. It is not always easy to discern between what is right and what seems right. And so, the Christian asks not so much, "Should I take my stand for, or against, this?" but rather, "Wherever I take my stand, am I standing with Jesus?"

Isn't that true?

For Further Discussion

1. What was the Via Maris, and what was its significance in the first century?
2. Typically today, if we build a new structure, we first clear away any older structures on the site before building the

new one. But ancient peoples built newer structures right on top of older ones. Why did they do that?

3. What was the significance of the octagonal shape for early Christians?

4. Why are archaeologists so sure that the octagonal structure discovered at Capernaum is the house of the apostle Simon Peter?

5. What is the significance of the biblical phrase "Galilee of the Gentiles"?

6. Why did Mark choose in his Gospel to portray Jesus primarily as an exorcist?

7. Why is spiritual discernment so important in our struggle with evil?

NOTES

1. James F. Strange and Hershel Shanks, "Synagogue Where Jesus Preached Found at Capernaum," *Biblical Archaeological Review* 9, no. 6 (1983): 25–31.

2. See J. N. D. Kelly, *The Epistles of Peter and of Jude* (New York: Harper and Row, 1969), 158–59. Kelly suggests that early Christian octagonal imagery is behind the reference to the "eight souls saved through water" in 1 Peter 3:20.

3. More precisely, Simon's wife's house, as Mark 1:29–31 (and parallels) indicates that Simon's mother-in-law "lay sick with a fever" in the house. Hence, the house was probably the home of Simon's wife and mother-in-law rather than of Simon, who, according to John 1:44, came not from Capernaum but from Bethsaida, on the easternmost corner of the Evangelical Triangle, along with his brother, Andrew, and two other disciples, Philip and Nathaniel. Simon probably made his mother-in-law's house his base of operations during the fishing season while fishing in the harbor near Capernaum.

4. Jack Finegan, *The Archeology of the New Testament: The Life of Jesus and the Beginning of the Early Church* (Princeton, N.J.: Princeton University Press, 1978), 56.

5. Ibid.

6. James F. Strange and Hershel Shanks, “Has the House Where Jesus Stayed in Capernaum Been Found?” *Biblical Archaeological Review* 8, no. 6 (1982): 29.

7. See Mark 1:29–39; 2:1.

8. A beautiful model of the synagogue and the house can be viewed at Gardner-Webb University in North Carolina, where it is on display in the Dover Memorial Library. The model, constructed by J. William McGehee, preserves the Capernaum Jesus knew as it would have appeared in the first century.

9. Frederick Buechner, *Wishful Thinking: A Theological ABC* (New York: Harper & Row, 1973), 19.

10. Ernest Campbell, *Locked in a Room with Open Doors* (Waco, Tex.: Word Books, 1974), 33–34.

CHAPTER 7

The Jordan River: Yardenit

North of the Huleh Basin, at the foot of Mount Hermon, at a place called Banyas (Caesarea Philippi of the New Testament), named for the Greek god Pan, lies the spring of Pan, one of the three sources of water for the Jordan River. The springs of Dan and the springs of the Bekka Valley are the other two sources of water that converge in the Huleh to form the headwaters of the Jordan. From there the river descends through the rift valley the twenty-five miles or so down to the lake known as the Sea of Galilee (see chapter 3). Exiting the lake on the south, the river reappears at a place known today as Yardenit.

Yardenit has been a Christian holy site since ancient times. Because the Jordan is readily accessible there, Yardenit has long been the place where Christian pilgrims have come to be baptized in the waters of the Jordan. A nineteenth-century painting depicts Christian pilgrims gathered at Yardenit to be immersed in the Jordan River. Since then, it has been a favorite spot for Christian baptismal services.

Today, Yardenit is maintained by a nearby Jewish agricultural commune, a *kibbutz.* Kibbutz Kenneret has transformed Yardenit into a modern, well-maintained, if somewhat touristy, setting for Christian baptisms. On most any day scores of Christians of all stripes from all around the world wade into the Jordan at Yardenit to be baptized, some for the first time, some to reaffirm their original baptism, some merely curious, some deeply moved. It is indeed a multicultural mosaic of Christian traditions. Yet, despite the diversity of languages, cultures, and liturgies, the baptisms witnessed at Yardenit have a curious familiarity about them irrespective of one's particular tradition, the wet-haired converts seeming more like brothers and sisters than strangers.

People choose to be baptized in the Jordan for all sorts of reasons. But many will attest to their desire to be baptized in the place where Jesus was baptized. Jesus, however, most certainly was not baptized at Yardenit, or nearby for that matter. Jesus, who was baptized by John the Baptist in the Jordan in identification with John's prophetic movement, was probably baptized some fifty miles or so south of Yardenit, near the mouth of the Dead Sea. It was there, rather than in the Galilee, that John the Baptist practiced his ritual cleansing immersions, called *mikvaoth,* as preparation for the coming of the kingdom of God, which he believed to be imminent. According to the Gospels, "the entire region of Judea and all the Jerusalemites" went out to the "wilderness" where John was baptizing in the Jordan River (Mark 1:4–5 and parallels). The reference to the wilderness of Judea places the location of John's activity, and therefore Jesus' baptism, nearer to Jericho than Yardenit. If indeed the local population went out to the wilderness to be baptized by the prophet, one would presume that John would have situated his place of baptism near the point on the river where people most frequently crossed it. In Jesus' day, the major path from Jerusalem to Jericho would have been through Wadi Qelt, which terminated at the Jordan at a ford in the river known as el-Hajlah. It was most likely here that John performed his *mikvaoth.*[1] The area today is part of the "no man's land" between Israel and Jordan, and therefore inaccessible to most tourists and pilgrims. And so, the Christian today really cannot be baptized where Jesus was baptized by John.

Moreover, contemporary Christian baptism not only happens at a place different from where Jesus was baptized, but also has a meaning profoundly different from his. The Gospels interpret the significance of Jesus' baptism as more coronation than conversion. The voice from heaven (*bath qol* in Hebrew) declared Jesus to be both son and servant of God (Mark 1:9–11 and parallels), son giving to servant a sense of identity, and servant giving to son a sense of purpose.[2]

For the Christian, however, baptism signifies a dying and rising with Jesus so as to embark on a whole new life and a whole new way of living in the world, which the New Testament describes as the kingdom of God. It is formation, not coronation, that the Christian's baptism signifies. It signifies an orientation to life so radical, so countercultural, so against the grain, that the New Testament can only describe it as death to an old way of life, and birth to a new. As William Willimon puts it, "Because the gospel is a way of thinking and being in the world that does not come naturally, we must be born again, and again."[3] So radical an event did baptism signify in the early church that converts were stripped stark naked, publicly immersed in the presence of the community of believers, and then, emerging from the "watery grave of baptism," given a new robe as a sign of their new status as members of the community of the baptized, and a new name to signify that the old person had died in the waters of baptism, and that the person who thus emerged arose to live a whole new life.

The Scripture: Romans 6:1–11

What, therefore, shall we say? "Let us continue in sin so that grace might abound"? Of course not! Those of us who have died to sin, how can we yet live in it? Or do you not know that as many of us as have been baptized into Christ Jesus were baptized into his death? We were buried, therefore, with him through baptism unto death, so that just as Christ was raised from the dead through the glory of the Father, so also we might walk in newness of life. For if we have been buried with him in the likeness of his death, we shall certainly be raised with him [in the likeness of his resurrection]. This we know: our old self was crucified with him so that the body of sin might be destroyed to the end that no longer should we be enslaved to sin. For the one having died has been set free

from sin. And if we have died with Christ, we believe that we shall also live together with him. For we know that Christ, having been raised from the dead, will never die, death no longer having authority over him. For the death he died he died to sin once for all; but the life he lives he lives to God. So also you shall consider yourselves to be dead to sin but alive to God in Christ Jesus.

"A Whole New Life"

My year in the fifth grade was a memorable one for me. I was ten years old that year, and that was the year I got "saved." That was what we called it back there in my little South Florida church—you got "saved." I remember hearing our pastor talk about how getting saved changed you, how everything was different after you got saved, that you got a whole new life in Christ. And so I spent a lot time following my baptism waiting for it to "hit" me. I went to school and told all my friends how I'd been saved, and how I was all different now. They couldn't see it. To them I looked pretty much the same, and acted pretty much the same, too.

I'd about decided my salvation didn't "take," when something happened to bring home to me pretty clearly how different this whole new life of mine was. You see, somewhere deep in the demonic bowels of the office of public instruction of Palm Beach County, Florida, it was decided that, instead of having the boys and girls go out to recess every day, it might be good to broaden the students' cultural horizons as well as to give them some physical activity. This, it was decided, could best be accomplished through square dancing.

Now I know that sounds pretty innocuous to you, but that shows just how much you know. You see, for Baptists in the South back in the 1950s, dancing—even square dancing—was just a shade shy of mass murder. Matter of fact, some believed it was worse! You could rehabilitate a mass murderer. But you let some poor unsuspecting fifth grader start dancing in school, and the next thing you know, he'll be frequenting honky-tonks and saloons before you can say "Bust a move!" You start down that road and it's "Derelict City"! I had visions of myself lying in the gutter, tattered clothes, hands clutching an empty wine bottle, and people coming by to stop and stare and say, "Wayne? Wayne Stacy? Is that you?" And then they'd lift my head to get a better look, and with my last, feeble words, I'd stammer, "But it was only *square dancing!*"

This was serious business. Furthermore, my father was a deacon in our church—taught the Wednesday night youth Bible study class, he did. We held to a different standard in our house. What would people think if the son of a deacon was seen square dancing in school, for heaven's sake? You can't have that. And so when I brought home the note from school informing my parents that square dancing would begin the following Monday, it was decided that I would "sit this one out." When I protested that everyone else would be square dancing, and so why couldn't I, my mother said, "That may be okay for them, but you're not them. You've been baptized—remember? You're a Christian now. You remember who you are." I remember wondering if Mormons danced.

Now I know that may sound silly to you and perhaps even a bit cruel, looking back on it today, but it was never my parents' intention to be cruel. It was a different time and a different place, and they were simply embracing as best they knew how what was to them a fundamental conviction: being Christian ought to mean something. To be sure, we might argue with them over where they chose to take their stand—majoring in minors, and all that—but they saw something clearly that's worth taking seriously, that there ought to be some difference between someone who is a Christian and someone who is not. To be sure, the execution may have been flawed and misguided, but the vision was valid. To be a Christian is to launch out on a whole new life.

For the earliest Christians, that vision was reflected in their baptism. As the late George Beasley-Murray, Baptist New Testament scholar and my teacher, compellingly demonstrated in his book *Baptism in the New Testament,* baptism for the first Christians was the sine qua non of faith. It was the moment when they "went public" with their faith. You might have been a "secret disciple" before baptism, but in the waters of baptism you declared yourself, you said to all who witnessed the act, "This is who I am. Any questions?"

It's unfortunate that in some denominations today, including my own, baptism has lost that "crossing over the line" significance it originally had. In my church, for instance, the very unbiblical sacrament of "walking the aisle" (i.e., coming forward at the end of a worship service to express a commitment to discipleship) now functions the way baptism originally did for the earliest Christians. But it was not always so.

Some years ago I got a feel for how baptism functioned among the first Christians when I was teaching at the Midwestern Baptist Theological Seminary in Kansas City, Missouri. I took a group of students to a small Caribbean island country for a missionary immersion experience as a part of a seminary course I was teaching. The little island country we visited was dominated at the time by an indigenous religion that was a rather strange mixture of Roman Catholicism, African tribal religions, and native superstitions. This curious coalescing of superstition and Christianity had a stranglehold on the indigenous population. To get a job, to buy a home, to register to vote, to be tolerated at all in the community, one had to be an active participant in the local religion; and to convert, to become a believer, meant risking everything. Needless to say, it was tough sledding for our missionaries there with whom the students and I worked. They were regarded with great suspicion, even open hostility.

After two weeks there with my students working among the nationals, we'd had some meager response. And so by the time the last Sunday rolled around, the missionary pastor had planned a dawn, oceanside baptismal service for the new believers. As he and I stood in the water that Sunday morning, about to baptize our first candidate, I noticed that the local townspeople had all gathered around on the beach to witness the event. It was remarkable, because at our previous services only a handful of the curious ever managed to show up. But here they were en masse to watch this baptism. I said to the missionary, "Isn't this great that all these people would come out to support their friends who are getting baptized today?" He looked at me and said, "They're not here because they want to support them; they're not even here because they're curious. They're here *taking names!*"

Taking names. In the early church, to be baptized was to go public, to cross the Rubicon, to declare yourself, who you are. So dramatic a moment, so irreversible the consequences, that in the early church, when people were baptized, they were stripped naked as the day they were born, plunged into the watery womb, and, when they emerged on the other side, to signify that they now had a whole new life, were given a new name.

It was, of course, from this ancient ritual that the practice of "christening" was born. Christening literally means "Christ-naming." "What name shall be given to this child?" the minister asks, and upon the child's baptism, the Christian name is bestowed. "Your Christian name shall be . . . "

Wayne or Catherine or Elizabeth or Thomas. Hear that? It's a defining moment, an ordaining moment, a "marking out" moment in which a whole new life is begun.

"That may be okay for them," she said, "but you're not them. You've been baptized. You have a whole new life now. And you have a new name. Your name now is 'Christian.' You remember who you are."

In his book *A Whole New Life,* Reynolds Price tells the story of his personal, spiritual struggle with cancer.[4] It took a tumor running down the length of his spine to remind him of what had always been true: we're all just a stroke or a tumor away from finding out who we really are.

"Six months to paraplegia, six months to quadriplegia, six months to death" was the sentence his old life had been given. In his words, he was leaning against a hard wind and scratching for bedrock in the oldest place he'd been taught to look, when the light broke through. Lying in bed early one morning about dawn, he found himself watching the sunrise, not in his bedroom, but on the slope of the Sea of Galilee, Lake Kenneret, where he'd visited twice before. Around him, lying in the grass, were Jesus' twelve disciples, still sleeping. So he lay there for a while in the early chill, the light a fine mix of tan and rose, looking west across the lake to Tiberias and north to Capernaum and Bethsaida.

Then one of the men woke and rose. It was Jesus, coming toward him. He bent over Price and said softly, "Follow me," and walked toward the lake. "I knew to shuck off my trousers and jacket," Price says, "then my shirt and shorts. Bare, I followed him." Waist deep in the water, Jesus took handfuls of water and poured them over Price's head and cancerous back. Then he spoke once. He said, "Your sins are forgiven." And that was it. He turned, leaving Price, with water running down his face and back, standing there in the lake alone.

Price called after him and said, in effect, "Uh, Lord, I don't want to seem ungrateful, but what about my cancer?" And Jesus turned and faced him and said just two words: "That too."

Price writes, "With no palpable seam in the texture of time or place, I was home again in my room." But though he was back, he was not the same. That experience in the waters of Kenneret became for him a defining moment, an ordaining moment, a naming moment in which he began, he says, a "whole new life, a life that's almost wholly changed from the old." Still bent, still broken, many challenges still ahead, but not the same person anymore.

Do you remember your baptism? That day you "took the plunge" and went public with your faith? That day Christ named you and marked you out as his very own?

Remember? That was the day you started a whole new life. And to mark that day, we gave you a new name. "From this day on, your name will be 'Christian,'" we said. "That's what we'll call you. Your name now is 'Christian.'"

It's a good name. It means "belonging to Christ."

That's who you are. That's *whose* you are. Don't forget it.

For Further Discussion

1. What did Jesus intend by his baptism at the hands of John the Baptist in the Jordan?

2. How is the Christian's baptism similar to Jesus'? How is it dissimilar?

3. What are the differences between what baptism meant for the first Christians and what baptism means for us in the church today?

4. Paul apparently believed baptism to signify such a radical transformation that he likened it to death and resurrection. Is that how most people today regard their baptism?

5. Many different modes of baptism are practiced by Christians today: immersion, sprinkling, pouring, even immersion of infants. In your opinion, how important is the mode of baptism?

NOTES

1. The traditional site of John's baptizing is a place near the Jordan River known as Deir Mar Juhanna, or the Monastery of St. John, about a mile or so south of the el-Hajlah ford.

2. The heavenly voice actually said, "You are my beloved son; with you I am well pleased" (Mark 1:11), but that New Testament statement is a conflation of two Old Testament messianic passages, Psalm 2:7 and Isaiah 42:1. The former identifies the messiah as God's son, and the latter, from the first Servant Song, identifies the messiah as the servant of the Lord.

3. William Willimon, *The Intrusive Word: Preaching to the Unbaptized* (Grand Rapids: Eerdmans, 1994), 34.

4. Reynolds Price, *A Whole New Life* (New York: Atheneum, 1994), esp. 42–43.

Part II

Bethlehem

CHAPTER 8

The Church of the Nativity

For Christians, there is no more sacred site in the world than the Church of the Nativity in Bethlehem. Standing in the center of the city, in the central plaza called Manager Square, the church is built on top of an ancient cave, the traditional site of the place where Jesus was born.

In the modern era, Bethlehem was a part of the country of Jordan, a Palestinian town of Christian and Moslem Arabs. Then, in the Six Day War of 1967, Bethlehem was successfully taken by Israel from Jordan, and the town became one of the occupied cities of the West Bank.

For the next thirty-one years Bethlehem languished as a Palestinian city controlled by a foreign occupational army. Poverty-ridden inhabitants eked out a meager living amid squalid surroundings and a hostile environment. In the 1980s in particular, Bethlehem was the site of much political unrest and uprising (*intifada* in Arabic). Little Bethlehem, as the prophet Micah had observed centuries earlier, really was "the least among the clans of Judah" (Micah 5:2).

But in January of 1998 things began to change. Israel vacated Bethlehem, along with five other West Bank towns, leaving it to the administration of the Palestinian Authority. Today, Bethlehem is back. A population of some thirty thousand persons, Bethlehem is in the midst of a building boom. Construction is everywhere. Again the markets are open and the shops busy. Bethlehem, the place of the Lord's birth, is itself being reborn.

The Church of the Nativity, as it appears today, is not at all what one would have expected. Resembling more a medieval fortress than a church, the Church of the Nativity is a sixth-century Byzantine basilica built over a fourth-century edifice constructed by Queen Helena, the mother of Emperor Constantine, in order to commemorate the site of an ancient cave that, since the days of Justin Martyr in the second century, had been associated with the birthplace of Jesus. Even today, many houses in Bethlehem are built in front of, and on top of, caves. The original fourth-century Church of the Nativity was built directly above such a cave, which from the earliest days had been associated with Jesus' birth. Under the church one can still visit the many, many caves of the cave complex that marks the site where Jesus entered our world. Moreover, the original church had an octagonal-shaped apse (dais) that was situated over a grotto traditionally associated with the cave of Jesus' birth. That the apse was octagonal lends further credence to the church's claim to authenticity, because the earliest Christians typically built their churches with eight sides—eight for the first day of the week, resurrection day.[1]

The Church of the Nativity one sees today is a Byzantine enlargement of Queen Helena's fourth-century church. It is the oldest church in Israel. Indeed, it survived the destruction of holy places during the seventh-century Turkish invasions of Palestine, in part because of a mosaic that once adorned the facade of the church—a mosaic depicting the visit of the magi to the baby Jesus, magi dressed in Persian garb. When the Turks saw the mosaic featuring prominent people who looked just like them, they spared the church.

When approaching the church, the first thing one notices is its austere, fortresslike quality. That reflects the period when the church, like most of Palestine, was contested by the Crusaders and the Turks. The sixth-century church originally had three doors leading to the narthex. During the brief Crusader occupation of Palestine (1099–1291), the two outer doors were walled up in order to make the structure easier to defend. The large central door was at that time reduced considerably in size to prevent marauding Turks mounted on horseback from entering through the great central door. Today, when entering the place where Jesus was born, one must pass through a little door that, appropriately enough, causes one to bend down very, very low.

The Scripture: Mark 10:13–16

And they were bringing children to him in order that he might touch them; but the disciples rebuked them. But Jesus, having

seen [them], became indignant and said to them, "Permit the children to come to me, and do not hinder them; for of such ones as these is the kingdom of God. Amen, I say to you, whoever does not receive the kingdom of God as a child should by no means enter into it." And having taken them into his arms, he blessed [them], putting his hands upon them.

"The Little Door"

Some years ago I was traveling in the Middle East with a group of student-tourists when we visited the Church of the Nativity in Bethlehem. Monitoring my group's entrance into the church, I stood at the door watching as one after another bent down very low to get through the little door. It was really quite a sight! I can't tell you how many people bumped their heads because they didn't bend down far enough. There's even a worn place in the portal where earlier pilgrims left their witness to the smallness of the little door. Tall students had to stoop especially low to go through the door. Older people, some of them no doubt arthritic, struggled to get low enough to get through the little door. For a full five minutes I just stood there and watched that little door "humble" people.

And all the while this was going on, there was this little Arab boy, just a child really, who couldn't have been more than five or six, hand outstretched, begging money from the tourists as they waited in line to go through the little door.

"Shekel? Shekel mister?" he asked. "You want to buy bookmark?" he asked others. He hit every single one before they entered. And then, when the last one in the group had successfully resisted his overtures, quick as a flash he darted through the door into the church to catch my group as they emerged on the other side and hit them up again.

"Shekel? Shekel?" he asked again, apparently undeterred by his earlier rebuff. I was amazed at how easily he negotiated the same door that had just humbled everybody in our group. He didn't even have to bend. You see, the door was sized perfectly for him. Everybody else had to struggle to get into this holy place, but not this little child. It was as though the entrance was made with him in mind. And I thought to myself, "What a cute little guy!"

It reminds me of something Jesus said when he wanted to give his disciples an object lesson about the nature of the kingdom of God. Jesus was busy preaching and teaching, and a large crowd had gathered around him. The crowd was responsive and Jesus was "on a roll." Before you knew it, he'd preached right through the lunch hour. The mothers, doing the best they could to keep the babies quiet, kept sticking the pacifiers in their babies' mouths, but that had long since served its usefulness. Finally, in a fit of frustration one of the disciples said, "Get the kids out of here. We're trying to get the kingdom going! How can we have the kingdom with all these babies screaming and crying?" And Jesus, hearing what the disciple had said, went ballistic (I'm paraphrasing, but you get the idea), and reaching into the crowd, he took a child in his arms and said, "No, no, no! Let the children come; don't stop them, because the kingdom of God looks exactly like this." And then to make sure they got the point, he added, "Now listen up [that's what "Amen, I say to you" really means]. Whoever does not receive the kingdom of God like a child will not enter into it."

This is no isolated word from Jesus. "I thank you, Father, that you have hidden these things from the wise and learned, and revealed them to little children" (Matthew 11:25). "I tell you the truth, unless you change and become like little children, you will never enter the kingdom of heaven" (Matthew 18:3). "Therefore, whoever becomes humble like this child is the greatest in the kingdom of heaven" (Matthew 18:4).

And that leads me to ask, What's the deal with kids and the kingdom? What is it about little children that makes them so apt a metaphor for the kingdom of God?

I don't know, really. It could be a lot of things, I guess. For example, maybe Jesus was just a good politician and knew instinctively that everybody loves children. Show me a politician who doesn't like babies and I'll show you a person who needs a job! Actors have a rule: "Never appear in a movie with a child or a dog. They'll upstage you every time!" When I dedicate babies in church, I walk down the aisle holding the little one, talking to it, telling it about the church it has become a part of, introducing the baby to its new spiritual family, and the family to its newest member. In the preparation for the event, the parents always express to me concern that their baby will misbehave or start crying during the ceremony and spoil it. I always tell them the same thing: "Hey, this is the only sure thing we do around here! The anthem may bomb, the sermon may go down in flames, but trust me on this one, everybody is gonna love your baby." Maybe that's it. I don't know.

Or maybe it's their innocence that Jesus was referring to. Children do go through life with an openness, an innocence that's appealing. Frederick Buechner, in his entry on "children" in his book *Wishful Thinking*, says, "[Children] are people who are so relatively unburdened by preconceptions that if somebody says there's a pot of gold at the end of the rainbow, they're perfectly willing to go take a look for themselves!"[2] Maybe that's it.

I know this: I've heard my share of sermons in my time on the virtues of "childlike faith." "If only we could believe like little children believe." Or "Children are so trusting. They don't ask for evidence or proofs; they just accept things." And it's usually at this point in the sermon that the preacher excoriates the evils of "too much learning" and the dangers of "seminary-trained preachers" who take the simple truths of the gospel and make them unnecessarily complex, presumably arguing for the value of ignorance over education. However, I would suggest that anyone who thinks faith is simple has never really believed anything, and that the ability of God to save the most ignorant measures the power of God, not the value of ignorance.

No. It's too easy to sentimentalize this text with a lot of mindless mush about children and miss Jesus' whole point here. At the risk of stating the obvious, let me remind you that Jesus here is not talking about children; he's talking about the *kingdom of God*. And the quality demanded for entry into the kingdom is the one quality children inherently possess—they're small.

Don't you see? Children are an apt metaphor for the kingdom because their egos are sized perfectly to get through its door. With children there is no feigned self-reliance or phony independence to balloon their egos to the size where entry into the kingdom is difficult. The kingdom of God is *God's* kingdom, not yours or mine or ours. In God's kingdom, *God* is sovereign, not you or me or us. And somehow, children not only know that instinctively, but they're also okay with it. They're perfectly willing to let God be God. They come to God with bareheaded, empty-handed, wide-eyed wonder. They have no sense of "having," only "needing," and that is precisely the posture required to gain access to God's kingdom—eyes up, hands empty and outstretched.

My friend Dr. Tony Cartledge, editor of the *Biblical Recorder,* tells a story about the cute and charming way his then two-year-old son, Samuel, had of expressing his desire for his dad to pick him up. Tony says that Samuel, like all little ones eager to communicate wants and wishes in ways that big people will respond to favorably, learned new words every day. Sometimes, he learned a new word for something just so he could ask for it! And in his mind he carefully put these words together in a way that, even if a bit muddled to adult ears, formed a kind of syntax that worked for him. And so when he wanted his dad to pick him up and hold him, he would hold out his chubby little arms and say, "I hold you me." With a simple and wonderful transparency that was neither self-conscious nor duplicitous, Samuel made his wish known to his daddy. It simply never occurred to him that this activity, which required the willing participation of another, could be something the other might not want to do. Note: there is no subtext, no hidden agenda, no ulterior motive, just "I hold you me." Now tell me you're going to resist that! Well, neither would God.

Don't you see? In the same way, to gain access to God's kingdom you must reach up. And if you're too big to reach up, then you must bend down very, very low.

C. S. Lewis once said,

> Until you have given up your self to Him you will not have a real self. . . . Does that sound strange? The same principle holds, you know, for more everyday matters. Even in social life, you will never make a good impression on other people until you stop thinking about what sort of impression you are making. . . . The principle runs through all life from top to bottom. Give up yourself, and you will find your real self. Lose your life and you will save it. . . . Nothing that you have not given away will be really yours. Nothing in you that has not died will ever be raised from the dead.[3]

"And a little child shall lead them" (Isaiah 11:6). I stood there in front of the Church of the Nativity that day looking at that little fellow running in and out of that little door as though it were made for him, and it suddenly occurred to me why this place, more than any other in all of Israel, holds such power over me. Because, you see, I keep looking for a Great, Big God who will make me stronger and wiser and smarter and bigger than I am. But in this place I encounter a different God—a God who is small and child-like and poor and weak, tugging at my sleeve, trying to get my attention, trying to lead me toward a kingdom with a very, very small door.

For Further Discussion

1. Why does the Church of the Nativity in Bethlehem resemble a fortress rather than a church?
2. Why did the Turks spare the Church of the Nativity during the Moslem invasions of the Holy Land in the seventh century?
3. Most scholars believe that the main entrance to the Church of the Nativity was lowered in order to prevent marauding Turkish soldiers on horseback from riding into the church through the front door. However, the little door also has the (unanticipated?) effect of causing worshipers to bend down in order to enter the church, an appropriate gesture when entering into the place where the King of kings was born. Which explanation seems more credible? Why?
4. How were children regarded in the ancient world?
5. What did Jesus mean when he said, "Whoever does not receive the kingdom of God like a child shall not enter into it"?

NOTES

1. See the discussion in chapter 6 on the house of Simon Peter at Capernaum.

2. Frederick Buechner, *Wishful Thinking: A Theological ABC* (New York: Harper & Row, 1973), 13.

3. C. S. Lewis, *Mere Christianity* (New York: Macmillan, 1979), 190.

CHAPTER 9

Shepherds' Field

The city of Bethlehem perches on a rocky ridge some 2,500 feet above sea level just to the south and west of Jerusalem. A city of over thirty thousand mostly Arab inhabitants today, Bethlehem sits atop terraced slopes on which farmers grow wheat, olives, and grapes, and on which shepherds graze flocks of sheep. Bethlehem lies on the ancient "Road of the Patriarchs," which was the major caravan route between Damascus and Egypt, winding its way through the Jezreel and Jordan Valleys. Passing through Jerusalem and Bethlehem on its way down to Hebron and points south, the road today is appropriately named "Hebron Road" as it makes its way through the city of Jerusalem. Bethlehem, whose name means "House of Bread," had a well-known caravansary, or inn, on the outskirts of the town, offering travelers a welcome respite from their grueling journeys.

Inns in the ancient world were not at all like our modern hotels and motels.[1] Built around a source of water, an ancient inn, referred to as a *katalyma* by Luke (2:7), offered a place where one might "loose down" one's animal for the night (*katalyma* literally means a "loosing down place"). An open courtyard where the animals were bedded for the night was surrounded on the ground floor by small stalls in which poorer travelers might lodge. A staircase led up to a second floor, where an open corridor led to a series of small, spartan rooms in which the more affluent could spend the night somewhat above the noise and smell of the courtyard below. In no case, however, did an ancient *katalyma* offer the kind of privacy to which we modern people have grown accustomed. Privacy was a luxury ancient peoples could rarely afford.

It is probably in this context that we are to understand Luke's oft-cited comment that Jesus was born in a manger "because there was no room for them in the inn." Raymond Brown's comments are worth noting:

> Most of the popular reflection on vs. 7 . . . misses Luke's purpose. Certainly irrelevant are speculations about why

> there was no room at the lodgings (influx of people for the census; presence of soldiers who took the census inscriptions; etc.), especially when these speculations lead to homilies about the supposed heartlessness of the unmentioned innkeeper and the hardship of the situation for the impoverished parents. As the Lucan narrative now stands, the manger does not signify poverty but a peculiarity of location caused by circumstances.[2]

Indeed, two seemingly insignificant comments that Luke makes suggest a very different scenario than the typical interpretation, which has a woman in the ninth month of pregnancy riding on a donkey eighty arduous miles and arriving virtually moments before giving birth, only to be turned away from lodging accommodations by a heartless innkeeper. First is Luke's statement, often ignored, that "while they were there, the days were accomplished that she should be delivered." This suggests that Joseph and Mary did not arrive on the afternoon of Jesus' birth, but may have been in Bethlehem some time prior to Mary's giving birth to Jesus. The second thing Luke says is that Jesus was bundled up and laid in a manger "because there was no room for them in the inn." However, the Greek word translated "room" is *topos*, and *topos* means "place" rather than "room," which is *monē* in Greek. That is, Luke did not say that Jesus was born in a manger because there was "no room" for them in the inn; rather, he says that Jesus was born in a manger because the inn was *no place* for them. The implication is that Joseph and Mary chose, probably with the innkeeper's assistance, a place more private in which Mary might give birth than an open and exposed *katalyma* could provide. According to very early traditions, what they came up with was a cave (the area around Bethlehem is percolated with limestone caves) that the local shepherds used as shelter for their flocks during the cold, wet, and often raw winter months (November through March). But, as Luke tells us, the shepherds were "out in the fields keeping watch over their flock by night," indicating that the shepherds were not using the cave shelters for their sheep and goats at that time of the year, thus making them available for Joseph and Mary's use. Indeed, the tradition that Jesus was born in a cave is so early and so strong that Constantine, in 325, built his famous church marking the site of the nativity over a network of caves in what would have been the outskirts of Bethlehem in the first century (see chapter 8).

Coincidentally, if Luke's description of events is correct, then Jesus could not have been born on December 25 or on any other winter night. Luke's description of the shepherds being "out in the fields with their flocks" means that Jesus must have been born sometime after March, when the rainy winter season had ended. Lambing season was in April, and lambs were not permitted into the fields until after the spring harvest so that they would not eat the crops. That Luke says that the flocks were "out in the fields" indicates that Jesus was born in late spring, probably late April or early May.

The fields now known as "Shepherds' Fields" are about two miles south of Bethlehem, nearer the Dead Sea and at a slightly lower elevation than Bethlehem, so as to make them below the snow line.[3] Beyond their historical reference, the presence of the shepherds had symbolic significance for Luke. Luke has deliberately placed the birth of Christ against the backdrop of the imperial claims of Caesar Augustus (see Luke 2:1–7). Standing like a colossus astride the greatest empire the world had ever known—one foot on land, one foot on sea—Augustus was the unrivaled king of the Greco-Roman world.

But Luke, reflecting on the ancient prophecies of Micah (4:8; 5:2) about a shepherd-king who would be a descendant of David, and who would be born up in Bethlehem, the city of David, whispers that with the birth of this tiny baby, Caesar, though he does not yet know it, is finished.

> And you, O tower of the flock [*migdal eder*],
> hill of the daughter of Zion,
> to you shall it come,
> the former dominion shall come,
> the kingdom of the daughter of
> Jerusalem. (Micah 4:8, RSV)

> But you, O Bethlehem Ephrathah,
> who are little to be among the
> clans of Judah,
> from you shall come forth for me
> one who is to be ruler in Israel,
> whose origin is from of old,
> from ancient days. . . .
> And he shall stand and feed his flock
> in the strength of the Lord,
> in the majesty of the name of the
> Lord his God.
> And they shall dwell secure, for now
> he shall be great
> to the ends of the earth. (Micah 5:2, 4, RSV)

Luke understands the Micah prophecy regarding the "tower of the flock" *(migdal eder)* to be a reference to Bethlehem, "hill of the daughter of Zion," from which the new shepherd-king will come, who will "stand and feed his flock in the strength of the Lord." In this regard, it is significant that the only other mention of the "tower of the flock" *(migdal eder)* in the Bible is in Genesis 35:19–21, where we are told that Rachel died and was buried on the road to Bethlehem (Ephrath), and that Israel (Jacob), journeying on from there, pitched his tent beyond *migdal eder,* that is, near Bethlehem.[4] Luke's reference, then, to shepherds out in the fields "tending their flocks" gathers up that old prophecy of Micah about the birth of a new shepherd-king in *Migdal Eder,* Bethlehem, the city of David, who will turn Caesar's world upside down and inside out.

That's why the baby is the "sign" for which the shepherds had been looking ("And this to you is a sign: you will find a baby swaddled and lying in a manger" [Luke 2:12]).[5] It's extraordinary, really, that the baby should be the sign and not the appearance of the heavenly hosts. With angels suddenly appearing in the night sky singing and praising God, how big a sign do you need? And yet, Luke says, *the baby,* quivering and puking in his mother's arms, is the sign! How strange. Perhaps that's why the birth of the shepherd-king caused hardly a ripple in the world Luke describes as the *oikoumenē,* "the whole inhabited world," technical language for the Greco-Roman empire over which Augustus ruled.

We have to face it: the birth of the Son of God went largely unnoticed in Caesar's world. But for a few shepherds out in the fields, most people were completely unaware that, with the birth of this tiny baby, the world as they had known it had just ended. But it had!

The Scripture: Luke 2:1–20

Now in those days a proclamation went out from Caesar Augustus to take a census of the whole inhabited world. This was the first census, and it occurred when Quirinius was governor of Syria. And all went to participate in the census, all to their own cities. And Joseph, too, went up from Galilee, out of the city of Nazareth, to Judea, to the city of David, which is called Bethlehem, because he was of the house and ancestry of David, to participate in the census with Mary, his betrothed, who was pregnant. And while they were there, the days of her pregnancy were completed,

and she delivered her son, the firstborn, and swaddled him and laid him in a manger, because there was no [appropriate] place for them in the inn.

And shepherds were in that area guarding and keeping the night watch over their flock. And an angel of the Lord appeared to them, and the glory of the Lord enveloped them, and they became terrified. And the angel said to them, "Fear not, for behold, I bring you good news of great joy which shall be to all people; for a Savior has been born in the city of David who is the Messiah, the Lord. And this is a sign to you: you will find a baby swaddled and lying in a manger." And suddenly a multitude of heaven's hosts appeared with the angel, praising God and saying, "Glory to God in the highest, and on earth peace among people of favor."

And as the angels departed into heaven, the shepherds were talking to one another: "Let us, then, go on to Bethlehem and see this thing that has happened which the Lord has made known to us." And hurrying, they came and found Mary and Joseph, and the baby lying in a manger. And having seen [it], they reported what had been told them concerning this child. And all who heard it were amazed concerning the things that the shepherds told them. But Mary guarded all these things, weighing [them] in her heart. And the shepherds returned glorifying and praising God for everything they had heard and seen, just as it had been told them.

"Angels We Have Heard Nearby"[6]

In his amazing book of short stories called *White People,* Allan Gurganus tells the story of an old woman, a widow whose sons now live far away, standing at the sink early one morning dressed in a tatty robe and doing the dishes she left from the night before.[7] She's gazing out the window while she does the dishes, looking everywhere and nowhere, when she happens to notice out of the corner of her eye something fall to the ground in her backyard.

There, out near the picnic table, lies something white, with wings, shivering as though it were cold. It wasn't.

"No way," she says. But when she looks again, there it is, plain as day, resting on its side on a bright air mattress of its own wings.

"Outer feathers are tough quills, broad at bottom as rowboat oars. The whole left wing bends far under. It looks hurt."

Though her arthritis slows her a bit, she hurries—if you can call it that—outside to investigate. She stoops, creaky, over what can only be a young angel, unconscious.

Quickly, she checks overhead, ready for what? Some TV news crew in a helicopter? She sees only a sky of the usual size, a Tuesday sky stretched between weekends. She allows herself to touch this thing's white forehead. She gets a mild electric shock. Then—odd—her tickled finger joints stop aching. They've hurt so long. A practical person, she quickly cures her other hand. The angel grunts but sounds pleased. His temperature's a hundred and fifty, easy, but for him, this seems somehow normal. "Poor thing," she says, and—careful—pulls his heavy, curly head into her lap. The head hums like a phone knocked off its cradle. She scans for neighbors, hoping they'll come out, wishing they wouldn't—both.

As her courage grows, she touches his skin. Feels hard and rough, like an ice tray that clings to everything it touches. But she also notices that with every touch, thirty-year-old pains leave her. Emboldened, she whispers to him her private woes: the Medicare cuts; the sons too busy to come by; the daughters-in-law not bad, but not so great either. They, too, seem lifted from her just by the telling. And with every pain healed, with every heartache vitiated, the angel seems rejuvenated too. Her griefs seem to fatten him like vitamins.

Regaining consciousness, he whispers to her, "We're just another army. We all look alike—we didn't before. It's not what you expect. We miss the other. Don't count so much on the next. Notice things here. We're just another army."

"Oh," she says, like she understands. She doesn't.

Then, struggling to his feet and stretching his wings, with one solemn grunt, he heaves himself upward, just missing the phone lines.

"Go, go," the old woman, grinning, points the way. He signals back at her, opened mouthed and left behind. First a glinting man-shaped kite, then an oblong of aluminum in the sun, a new moon shrunk to the size of a decent-sized star, a final fleck of light, and then a memory, Tuesday memory.

What does she do? Whom does she tell? Who'll believe her? She can't tell her neighbor, Lydia. She'd phone the old woman's missing sons: "Come right home. Your mom's inventing . . . company!"

She hears the neighbor's collie barking frantically in the distance. (It saw!)

Maybe other angels have dropped into other backyards, she wonders. Behind fences, did neighbors help earlier ones? Folks keep so much of the best stuff quiet, don't they?

Regaining her aplomb, she bounces back inside to finish her dishes. Slowly, she notices, her joints start to ache again. The age spots that had totally vanished only moments before start to darken again. Everything is as it was before. Well, not everything.

Standing there at the sink, she seems to be expecting something. Look at her, crazy old woman, staring out at the backyard, nowhere, everywhere. She plunges her aching hands in the warm, soapy water and whispers, "I'm right here, ready. Ready for more."

An old woman, who seems to be washing dishes, but she's not. She's guarding the world. Only, nobody knows.

Seen any angels lately? I have. Well, let me rephrase that. I've seen a lot *about* angels lately, and in the strangest places.

Some time ago, NBC television did a two-hour special, hosted by Patty Duke, called "Angels: Those Mysterious Messengers." Two-hours! Imagine, a commercial television network devoting two hours of prime time to angels!

CBS, not to be outdone, has had a successful run with its prime-time program about angels who visit earth on a mission from God. *Touched by an Angel* has been one of the most successful television programs in recent years.

And then there was this feature article in *USA Today* about guardian angels. The story was about the current practice, popular among many, of wearing little guardian angels on their lapels. You've seen them too, huh? Apparently, many believe that there's more to life than meets the eye.

Time magazine devoted the cover of its December 1993 issue to angels. Inside, the feature article, "Angels Among Us," trumpeted (sorry about that!) the statistic that 69 percent of Americans polled said that they believed in angels.

And in an issue of the *Ladies Home Journal*—I don't read it myself, mind you, but I know people who do—there was another article about guardian angels, stories about people who, they believed, were miraculously delivered from all kinds of difficulties, people who sincerely believe it was angels who made the difference.

Unless you're hiding under a rock, you'll hardly make it through the Christmas season without seeing yet again the marvelous, if not altogether competent, angel Clarence, in Frank Capra's classic movie *It's a Wonderful Life*.

And Frederick Buechner says of angels: "Sleight-of-hand magic is based on the demonstrable fact that as a rule people see only what they expect to see. Angels are powerful spirits whom God sends into the world to wish us well. Since we don't expect to see them, we don't. An angel spreads his glittering wings over us, and we say things like 'It was one of those days that made you feel good just to be alive' or 'I had a hunch everything was going to turn out all right' or 'I don't know where I ever found the courage.'"[8]

Seen any angels lately? Well, the Bible has. Apparently without even the decency to be embarrassed, the Bible speaks of a world populated with angels. Abraham and his aging wife, Sarah, entertain three visitors among the oaks of Mamre, who reveal to them that they will have a son. When the bewildered old couple protests that this sounds too good to be true, the "visitors" ("some have entertained angels unawares" [Hebrews 13:2]) say, "Is there anything too hard for God?" Jacob wrestles by the brook Jabbok with an angel in human disguise. Samson's father, Manoah, carried on a conversation with a messenger, completely unaware until after the messenger had disappeared that he had been talking to an angel.

And in the New Testament, angels accompany critical events in the life of Jesus and the church. They announce his birth, minister to him after his temptation, announce his resurrection, and attend his ascension. And they assist the fledgling church at crucial times, aiding the apostles in persecution, assisting with the spread of the gospel to the Gentiles, rescuing Paul and Silas from a Philippian jail.

The word "angel" means "messenger"—*malakh* in Hebrew, *malak* in Arabic, *angelos* in Greek—and more often than not, that's how angels function in the Bible, as messengers of God. They were not a part of Jewish theology in its earliest development. Early on, Israel had thought of its God as being a very immanent, personal, even anthropomorphic God, walking and chatting with Adam in the garden in the cool of the day. But later on, this immanent concept of God gave way to a more transcendent idea of God—distant, unapproachable, removed from creation. And so, probably under the influence of their neighbors, Israel's theologians posited angels as intermediary beings between God and creation, facilitating communication between the

Almighty and creatures. They were given special assignments as guides or messengers or caretakers, and certain ones had names, such as Michael or Gabriel. In some ancient texts, angels were thought to be the personification of stars, the heavenly hosts of God, the "army of God" who accompanied God in battle against all the cosmic forces arrayed against the Almighty. In the book of Judges, the song of Deborah celebrates Israel's victory over the Assyrian king Sisera as a victory of Israel's God, YHWH, over the hostile cosmic forces: "From heaven fought the stars; from their courses they fought against Sisera" (Judges 5:20).[9]

"We're just another army," he said. Coming out of late Judaism, Christianity was from the start influenced by the widespread belief in angels and demons. And so, it's not at all surprising that when Luke gets to the part of his story where the birth of the Messiah is to be announced to unsuspecting shepherds out tending their flocks in the fields, the messengers are angels.

Seen any angels lately? Don't be too disappointed if you haven't. Not everyone believes in angels.

Some biblical scholars disbelieve in angels, at least as spiritual beings. They find it hard to buy into all the mumbo jumbo about ghosts and spirits and angels and such. I have to admit that there was a time when I disbelieved in a spiritual world. I thought it was an anachronistic residue of a more primitive age in which the world was populated with spiritual, incorporeal beings who could pass through solid objects and could suddenly appear and disappear, as angels do throughout Scripture. I thought such a world belonged to fairy tales and children's books, with their trolls and enchanted creatures. But having read C. S. Lewis's marvelous book *The Great Divorce,* I'm not so sure anymore. You see, he says that perhaps we've got it backward. Rather than angels being insubstantial and translucent, able to pass through solid objects because they have no substance, what if it's the reverse! What if it is we who are insubstantial and incorporeal relative to their world, and it is they, not we, who are so solid, so dense, that they pass through what we regard as solid objects as though they were merely a mist or a fog? "Earth," Lewis says, "is the grey town with its continual hope of morning."[10]

I don't know.

Because the word "angel" simply means "messenger," some scholars believe that angels may not be spiritual beings at all, but anybody who brings a message from God. There is some precedence for this view. The Old Testament book of Malachi takes its title from the Hebrew word *malakhi,* meaning "my messenger," referring to the prophet as a messenger of God. But, of course, the word *malakh* can also be translated "angel." Was Malachi a prophet or an angel?

I don't know. And I don't know who knows.

I know this: Sometimes God sends messages to us in some pretty unusual packaging, and if we're not attentive, if we're not looking, if we're not listening, we can miss them.

A friend of mine was preaching a revival recently, and because of some pressing business back at his office, he was traveling back and forth to the church every evening for the services. By the end of the week he was pretty tired.

One night, as he was traveling home, he stopped at a convenience store to get a cup of coffee to steel himself for the long drive ahead. It was late, and he was tired as he came out of the store. As he walked to his car, an old man came up to him and asked him if he had any spare change to give. Well, as I said, it was late, and my friend was tired and wanted to get home. And besides, you can't be too careful, can you? Can you? And so my friend said, "No," with his hands on some quarters in his pocket.

The next night at the church, a lady came up to him and told him that as a result of his sermon the night before she had been moved to give a man some spare change from her purse. She said, "You never know, maybe God sent him my way?"

Do you think . . . maybe . . . he was . . . ? Nah.

But even so, I can't forget what the writer of Hebrews said: "Don't you neglect to show hospitality to strangers, for thereby some have entertained angels unawares!"

Have you seen any angels lately?

John Duckworth did. He tells a story about Pastor Torgenson, who stood before his congregation as they gathered one cold Christmas Eve for a Christmas Eve testimony service.[11] It was their custom in that little church every Christmas Eve to celebrate Christmas by sharing with each other how God had blessed them during the previous year.

And so, as the people gathered, Pastor Torgenson began: "Before the choir sings 'Angels We Have Heard on High,' let me remind you of a Scripture passage about angels. Turn to Hebrews 13:2."

A tissue-thin shuffle of Bible pages went through the sanctuary and then was rudely interrupted as a haggard couple entered the back. The man had a bushy beard and old, faded clothes. She was pregnant and wore a tattered dress.

"Wonder if they're even married?" someone murmured.

"Well, I never. . ." said another.

Old Mizzie Everett just squinted, apparently as confused as ever. Pastor Torgenson smiled and invited them to find a seat. It wasn't easy. The church was full, it being Christmas Eve and all. They had to make their way all the way down front.

Then, Pastor Torgenson read those verses, you know, about entertaining angels unawares. He himself was surprised at the timing of it all, this young couple showing up unexpectedly like that.

After the choir sang, he invited people in the congregation to give their testimonies.

"Anyone want to share a brief word of testimony?" He had emphasized "brief" on account of Old Mizzie. My, the way she could carry on about nothing! Trying to remember dates, singing with an awful squeal. Folk just kind of shook their heads, chuckled under their breath, and said, "Well, you know Old Mizzie."

Sure enough, Mizzie was the first to the microphone. You could almost hear the unspoken "Ahhhh." True to form, she went on and on, with Pastor Torgenson politely interjecting, from time to time, "Thank you very much, Mizzie," as though that would stop her. It didn't. Finally, finally, she was through.

Then, the haggard young man rose. "I don't know nothin' 'bout talkin' in church," he began, "but me and my ol' lady—uh, my wife—we really need a place to stay. I ain't got no job."

When he finished, Pastor Torgenson commented, "We appreciate your sharing with us. I think we can help. By the way, what's your name?"

"I'm Joe. She's Mary."

You could see the congregation's wheels turning—*Joseph and Mary*? Come on, now!

"Yeah, I know how it sounds. Really, though."

In the fellowship time later, a good number of folks talked with the young couple while nibbling on cookies. Several offered places to stay and one of the men talked to Joe about a job. Old Mizzie stood in the corner, ignored, sipping coffee and nibbling on a cookie.

Suddenly, she looked at her watch, put down her coffee cup, and started for the door. She mounted her three-wheel bike and began pedaling slowly back outside of town. The night air was cold, and her old body was so worn. When she reached the edge of town, she stopped near an empty field. The highway was deserted. Only the stars and heaven watched as she climbed the sloping hill. A dog barked in the distance.

"Christmas Eve," she said to herself. "Just like that first Christmas Eve when we sang of his birth. That was easy compared to this assignment! Well, time to go home now."

She smiled, closed her eyes, and reached heavenward. "Goin' home," she whispered, "goin' home."

How's that go again? "Angels We Have Heard *Nearby*"? Who knows? "Is there *anything* too hard for God?"

Seen any angels lately? Are you . . . are you sure?

For Further Discussion

1. How have our contemporary understandings and ideas influenced the way in which we tell the Christmas story?

2. Why was it to shepherds that the announcement about the birth of Jesus was first disclosed?

3. Why have Christians come to celebrate December 25 as the birthday of Christ even though it is likely that he was born in the spring rather than in the winter?

4. The writer of Hebrews talks about the possibility of "entertaining angels unawares" (Hebrews 13:2). Have you ever had any experiences that you might describe that way?

NOTES

1. See Raymond E. Brown, *The Birth of the Messiah* (Garden City, N.Y.: Doubleday, 1977), 400–401.

2. Ibid., 418–19.

3. Ibid., 401.

4. The traditional site of the tomb of Rachel, site of recent skirmishes between Hasidic Jews from Jerusalem and the indigenous

Arab population of Bethlehem, stills lies on the old "Road of the Patriarchs" just outside Bethlehem. For the view that the "tower of the flock" is a reference to Jerusalem rather than Bethlehem, see Brown, *Birth of the Messiah,* 422.

5. Swaddling was not merely to protect the newborn from the cold; it also was a method of restricting the infant's movements to insure that the child's arms and legs would grow straight. For the first six months of life, the infant was swaddled, being loosed only once a day for bathing, the mother rubbing on olive oil and powder made of dried myrtle leaves to prevent chafing. Swaddling is still used today in some parts of the world. See Kaari Ward, ed., *Jesus and His Times* (Pleasantville, N.Y.: Reader's Digest Association, 1987), 22–23.

6. A version of this homily was first published in *The Library of Distinctive Sermons,* ed. Gary W. Klingsporn (Sisters, Oreg.: Multnomah, 1997), 6:79–93. Reprinted by permission.

7. The story that follows is an adaptation of "It Had Wings," by Allan Gurganus, in *White People: Stories and Novellas* (New York: Ballantine Books, 1992), 162–66.

8. Frederick Buechner, *Wishful Thinking: A Theological ABC* (New York: Harper & Row, 1973), 1–2.

9. For a brief but excellent treatment of the function of angels in the Bible, see Dale C. Allison Jr., "What Was the Star that Guided the Magi?" *Bible Review* 9, no. 6 (December 1993): 20–24.

10. C. S. Lewis, *The Great Divorce* (New York: Macmillan, 1979), 38.

11. John Duckworth, "Angels We Have Heard on High," in *Stories That Sneak Up on You* (Grand Rapids: Fleming H. Revell, 1987), 154–59.

Part III

Jerusalem

CHAPTER 10

The Cenacle: The Upper Room of the Last Supper

The city of Jerusalem stands about 2,700 feet above sea level. The Jerusalem of today is divided into two distinct sections, the modern western section and the ancient eastern section, which includes the Old City, the Mount of Olives, the Arab town of Silwan (biblical Shiloh), the Ophel (ancient City of David), and

Mount Zion. East Jerusalem sits atop a rocky plateau surrounded on three sides by rather precipitous gorges, called in Hebrew, *gayim.*[1] The gorge *(gay)* that borders Jerusalem on the south and west is known as the gorge of Hinnom, or *gay hinnom,* that is, Gehinnom (biblical Gehenna of Matthew 5:29, etc.). The gorge that surrounds Jerusalem on the east is significantly smaller and shallower, and is not really a gorge at all, but rather a *nahal* (Hebrew), or *wadi* (Arabic), a narrow ravine that suddenly fills with torrents of water during the rainy winter season. A shallower, narrow valley, referred to by the Jewish historian Josephus as the Tyropoeon Valley, or "Valley of the Cheesemakers," divides the plateau of Jerusalem into two distinct ridges, eastern and western.

Of the two, the western is the higher. The western ridge is also bisected by a smallish, shallow transverse valley that runs from west to east and terminates in the Tyropoeon Valley near the Western Wall, commonly called the Wailing Wall. This small valley divides the western ridge into two parts, north and south. Sitting atop the northern peak of the western ridge is the Church of the Holy Sepulchre (see chapter 11). But the southern peak of the western ridge is the higher and is, indeed, the highest peak in the Old City. It is for this reason that the southwestern peak came to be identified in early Christian tradition with the biblical Mount Zion.

Today, Mount Zion is located outside the southwest wall of the Old City. Tradition has it that its location outside the walls was a mistake. The story is that in the sixteenth century, when Suleiman the Magnificent ordered the walls of the Old City to be rebuilt, his engineers neglected to include the peak in their calculations and were summarily executed for their oversight.

In any case, Mount Zion is considered holy by Jews and Christians alike. Today, a complex of buildings stands on Zion, including the Church of the Dormition,[2] Dormition Abbey (Benedictine), the Tomb of David (traditional site),[3] the Mosque of the Prophet David (Moslem), and, in the second story of the building that houses the Tomb of David, the traditional site of the upper room, or the room of the Last Supper, known as the Cenacle (from the Latin *cenaculum,* by which Jerome rendered the Greek word for "upper room," *anagaion,* in Mark 14:15 and Luke 22:12).

The Cenacle is only the traditional location where Jesus, according to the Synoptic Gospels (Matthew, Mark, and Luke), celebrated the Passover Seder (ceremonial meal) with his disciples on the night of his betrayal and arrest (Mark 14:12–31 and parallels).[4] Virtually no one considers this site to be authentic, though the physical location of the room is certainly plausible.[5] The present room, which dates only to the fourteenth century, is a large, empty chamber with Gothic arches and early Christian bas relief carvings on the capitals of the pilasters. It bears little, if any, resemblance to the upper room described by Mark.

But whether the Last Supper occurred here or somewhere else, the story of Jesus' rather secretive supper with his disciples on his last night with them is curious indeed. As Mark 14:12–31 narrates it, Jesus, on the first day of the Feast of Unleavened Bread (the feast leading up to the Passover), instructed his disciples to go into the city (and that means inside the walls of the city of Jerusalem) and find and follow a man carrying a water jar to a house somewhere in an undisclosed location in the city. When confronted at the door by the householder, they were to say, "The Teacher says, 'Where is my guest room [*katalyma*] where I am to eat the Passover with my disciples?'" Then, the householder would lead them to a large upper room *(anagaion)*, furnished and ready, where they were to prepare the Passover meal for later that evening. Strange.

Why all the secrecy? Why were they to describe Jesus to the householder by means of the rather cryptic title "the Teacher"? And how, among all the hosts of people in the city at Passover, were they to find the one man carrying a water jar who would be the very person who would lead them to the right upper room for their Passover meal? And perhaps most difficult of all, why is it that the Synoptic Gospels describe Jesus' Last Supper with the disciples as a Passover meal, when the Gospel of John says that the Passover lambs were in the process of being slaughtered in preparation for the eating of the Passover at the very time that Jesus was being arraigned and crucified (John 19:14–16), implying that Jesus' Last Supper with the disciples could not have been the Passover?

The famous Dead Sea Scrolls may provide some answers. For example, Jesus and his disciples had to form something of a secret society for the same reason the Essenes (the Dead Sea Scrolls community) had to form one: the Roman occupational army saw them as subversive and potentially revolutionary. Both Jesus and his disciples and the Essenes of Qumran had formed themselves into a messianic community outside the bounds of official Judaism, which they rejected because of the latter's capitulation to and collaboration with the pagan occupational army. It should not be missed that while Jesus' frequent controversies were with the Pharisees, it was the Sadducees in collaboration with the Romans, not the Pharisees, who were responsible for

Jesus' death—about that the Gospels are clear. The Sadducees ran the temple and were the wealthy, landed gentry of the day who had gained the most from the economic stability that the Romans had brought to Palestine, and who had the most to lose from a messianic revolt among the populace. The Essenes, in a protest against the corruption of the Sadducees, had moved out to the shores of the Dead Sea, there in isolation and seclusion to practice their messianic Judaism and to look forward to the day when God would raise up the Messiah to rid the land of the hated Romans and their corrupt Jewish collaborators (both of whom they referred to in their writings as "Sons of Darkness"). While Jesus was not a seditionist, he certainly agreed with the Essenes that the Sadducees and their trickle-down temple economy had failed to live up to their God-given responsibility of keeping the people connected to God (cf. Jesus' cleansing of the temple in Mark 11:15–17 and parallels). Especially in the wake of Jesus' protest demonstration in the temple, both the Romans and the Sadducees would have regarded Jesus and his disciples to be an Essene-like group of potential revolutionaries and would have kept an eye on them as possible troublemakers, especially at Passover, when messianic Jewish fervor always ran high. And so, it is not at all surprising that Jesus and his disciples decided to maintain a very low profile during the Passover festivities.

And what of the man carrying the water jar? In that culture, then and now, carrying water was a task reserved for women. Men didn't carry water jars unless, of course, they happened to be a part of an all-male monastic community, where there were no women to do these chores, such as the Essenes, or Jesus and his disciples. Thus, a man carrying a water jar through the crowded streets of Jerusalem would have stuck out like the proverbial sore thumb. It would not have been difficult at all to find such a person and follow him through the narrow streets to the one house where the guest room had been readied.

And why were they to refer to Jesus as "the Teacher"? Interestingly enough, the favorite designation for the leader of the Essenes was the Teacher, or more specifically, the Teacher of Righteousness. To refer to someone such as Jesus, a messianic Jewish leader who was gathering a messianic community in anticipation of the kingdom of God, as the Teacher would have been normal and natural among Essene-like communities of messianic Jews such as Jesus and the Twelve.

And finally, what of the differences between John and the Synoptics over the date of the Last Supper and the crucifixion? Once again, reference to the Dead Sea community of Essenes offers help. As a protest against the corruption of the Sadducees, the Essenes followed a calendar for religious festivals that differed from the one preferred by official Judaism as administered by the Sadducees in Jerusalem. The Essenes followed a solar calendar for religious festivals such as Passover, rather than the lunar calendar employed by the Sadducees in Jerusalem. Indeed, one of the books found among the Dead Sea Scrolls was the book of Jubilees, which is a commentary on religious feasts and festivals employing the solar calendar. Hence, we know that the Essenes were studying the solar calendar at Qumran and preferred it to the lunar calendar of official Judaism. This meant, among other things, that their festivals fell on different dates than the dates on which those same festivals were being observed in Jerusalem. If Jesus and his disciples were indeed organized as an Essene-like protest community of messianic Jews, then they too would have observed their festivals, such as Passover, on different dates than those observed by mainstream Jews in Jerusalem. This probably is the reason that the Synoptics and John differ on the date of Jesus' Last Supper and his crucifixion. The Synoptics, you see, are giving an "insider" description of the events, and from the point of view of Jesus and his disciples, it was indeed Passover, and the Last Supper was a Passover meal. However, from the point of view of official Judaism, from which vantage point John tells the story, Passover had not yet been observed when Jesus gathered with his disciples in the Cenacle; rather, it would occur sometime later, when Jesus was being arraigned and crucified, a fortuitous coincidence for John in that he interprets Jesus' death as something of a Passover sacrifice anyway.

In any case, when Jesus gathered with the Twelve in the Cenacle to break bread and drink wine, it would be his "last" supper with them. Or would it?

The Scripture: Luke 24:13–35

And behold, two of them on that day were going to the village named Emmaus, about seven miles from Jerusalem. And they were talking to one another concerning all these things that had transpired. And while they were talking and conversing, Jesus himself, having drawn near, joined them. But their eyes were kept from recognizing him. And he said to them, "What is this you're talking about while you're walking?" And they stopped and looked sad. And one of them, named Cleopas, answered and said to him, "You must be the only one living in Jerusalem who doesn't know what happened there the other day." And he said to them, "What things?" And they said to him, "The things concerning Jesus of Nazareth, who was a prophet mighty in word and deed before God and all the people, and how our chief priests and rulers delivered him unto the judgment of death and crucified him. And we had hoped that he was the one who was about to liberate Israel, but alas, [it was not to be]. And

besides all this, it is now the third day since this happened. What is more, some women from among us amazed us; having gone early in the morning to the tomb and not finding his body there, they returned saying that they had seen an appearance of angels who told them that he was alive. Some of our group went to the tomb and found [it] just as the women had said, but him they did not see." And he said to them, "O foolish and slow of heart to believe all the prophets spoke, were not these things necessary, that the Messiah should suffer and [then] enter into his glory?" And beginning with Moses and all the prophets, he interpreted to them in all the scriptures the things concerning himself.

And having drawn near to the village to which they were going, he seemed to be going [on] further. And [so] they constrained him saying, "Remain with us, for it is toward evening and the day is already far spent." So he went in to remain with them. And it happened that when he was reclining with them [at table], having taken bread, he blessed and broke it and gave it to them. And their eyes were opened and they knew him, and he disappeared from their sight. And they said to one another, "Did not our hearts burn within us as he was speaking to us on the road, when he opened to us the scriptures?" And having arisen that same hour, they returned to Jerusalem and found the eleven and those who were with them assembled saying, "Truly, the Lord has risen and has appeared to Simon!" And they told them the things [that happened] on the road, and how he had become known to them in the breaking of the bread.

"The Presence in the Absence"[6]

Some time ago, I got home in the evening and found the house empty. Our son, who was seventeen years old at the time, was at football practice, and my wife had left a note on the counter reminding me that she had a commitment and would not be home until later.

"Dinner is on the stove," she had written. "Your favorite—spaghetti. Enjoy!" I chuckled under my breath, helped myself to a plateful, and sat down alone at the little table in the kitchen to eat my supper. I chuckled because she called spaghetti my "favorite." It's an inside joke. You see, when my wife and I were first married, the first thing she ever cooked for me was spaghetti. It was very "interesting" spaghetti, shall we say? My wife has since become an excellent cook, but it was not always so. She had not done much cooking growing up at home, and those first few meals after we were married were an "adventure," to say the least.

Now, let's be honest. Like any story, the story of my wife's now infamous spaghetti has grown through the years, but it was memorable.

It was another place and another time, but I came home to find my new bride looking somewhat panicked but trying not to let it show, busily stirring some white, stringy things in a pot on the stove. She said reassuringly, "Just sit down, honey, and read the paper. Dinner will be ready shortly." She said it like she knew what she was doing, so I smiled, sat down, and pretended to read the paper. But a growing sense of dread began to envelop me.

I noticed that she kept sticking her fork into the pot, taking out individual strands of spaghetti and looking at them as though they were somehow more interesting than I had ever before considered spaghetti to be. After a while, she looked at me and said, "Uh, do you know how to tell when spaghetti is done?"

I had to admit that in all my years of eating spaghetti, I never once gave the question a single moment's thought. Then, it hit me—something I'd seen my sister do when she was cooking spaghetti. I said, "Sure!" I walked over to the pot, reached in with the fork, and took out a single strand of the spaghetti; when it cooled enough for me to handle, I picked it up and promptly threw it at the cabinets. Plop! It stuck right there. I said, "It's done," and I walked back over to the table, sat down, and began to read the paper again.

You know, wives get upset about the least little things, don't they? I mean, I thought she was going to kill me!

"What are you doing?" she asked.

"Testing the spaghetti," I responded.

"For what, building materials?"

"Isn't that the way everybody tests spaghetti?"

"Most people eat spaghetti; you're the only one who throws it!"

It was getting dark as I sat alone in the kitchen eating that plateful of spaghetti, but all of a sudden I found myself laughing out loud, remembering that first encounter with spaghetti long ago and far away. It was already too late to retrieve them when I looked across the empty table and let loose the words "Do you remember that time when we cooked spaghetti?"

I thought, "This is silly. I'm talking to myself." I was alone. There was nobody there. But as I ate, somehow I knew that though no one was sitting at table with me, I really was sharing that plateful of spaghetti!

Has that ever happened to you? It happened to the early church every time they sat down together to eat the Lord's Supper. That's really what this story's about here in Luke: "the presence in the absence."

I know, I know, you thought that this story was an Easter story, not a communion story. And it's true. It starts out being an Easter story. Two lonely and disillusioned disciples of the crucified Jesus were walking along on the road from Jerusalem to Emmaus, discussing the events of the past few days, when suddenly a stranger appears with them. It's Jesus, but they don't know it.

"What are you talking about?" he asks them.

"Have you been hiding under a rock?" they answer.

"No, really, what are you guys talking about?" And so for the benefit of the stranger—and our benefit too, because we've also joined them on that walk to Emmaus—Cleopas and the other guy tell Jesus and us what's happened. Kind of a "flashback," you know.

Well, it gets late, and so sensing that this stranger has no place to go for supper, they invite him—and us—in to eat. But just about the time we all get settled around the table, something begins to happen. What started out as an ordinary meal, an act of hospitality to a stranger, becomes Communion with the risen Christ!

Listen to how Luke describes the seating at the meal. "When he was reclining at table with them. . . ." Did you get that? *Reclining* at table with them—that's what the Greek says. You don't recline at table for an ordinary meal. Only at Jewish festival meals, like Passover, did Jews recline, just as Jesus had done with his disciples just a few days earlier when he shared the "Last Supper" with them. Get it?

And listen to how Luke describes the serving of the meal. "And he took bread, and blessed and broke it, and gave it to them." "Took . . . blessed . . . broke . . . gave. . . ." Sound familiar?

And when did Jesus become the host at this supper? I thought he was the guest. And yet, when they join him at table, what started as supper ends as sacrament. The presence of the risen Christ turns an ordinary meal for a hungry stranger into a sacrament of the grace of God.

And that's Luke's point: every time believers gather at table in Christ's name, he'll be there! He's the "presence in the absence." Notice that Luke says, "They recognized him when he broke the bread with them." Now, Jesus had just spent considerable time explaining to them who he was by interpreting the Scriptures to them, and yet they didn't recognize him. They didn't have a clue who he was. But then they broke bread with him, and bingo! "It's Jesus!" And then they say, "Didn't our hearts burn within us when he opened to us the scriptures?" They most certainly did not! They didn't even recognize him when he was interpreting the Scriptures to them! But somehow, the experience at table made it all clear.

Do you see what Luke is doing? He's reminding his church—and ours—that stories about the risen Christ alone aren't sufficient to convince anybody of Christ's presence. Cleopas and his companion actually walked and talked with him, and didn't know him. They were eyewitnesses to the resurrection, and yet they didn't know what they'd witnessed.

And neither is the Scripture alone adequate to reassure us of the risen Lord's continued presence among us. After all, resurrection stories and even the Scriptures are ultimately witnesses to *somebody else's* experience with the risen Christ. Were that the whole story, all believers except those select few would experience only the absence of Jesus, fated to trying to keep faith alive on a thin diet of reports of somebody else's experience with him. Luke's church—and ours—would be relegated to being secondhand Christians, living on a secondhand faith.

But at table he's available to all of us, no matter when or where we live. Even in the absence there's a presence. Can't you feel it? Taste the bread; drink the cup. He's here! He's here! "And when he took bread, and broke it and blessed it and gave it to them, they recognized him."

There is, you see, something about you and me that needs to taste for ourselves to know for sure. Knowing is more than seeing; it's also doing. Father Divine used to say, "We preachers need to spend less time 'metaphysicalizing' and more time 'tangibilitating.'" I don't know why it's true—maybe the epistemologists can tell us—but it's true that an indissoluble link exists between knowing and doing.

Truth that really is true, for me, has a corporeality about it—it smells true; it tastes true; it feels true.

In medicine, the dictum is "See one; do one; teach one." I always used to tell students in my Greek classes that you don't really know a foreign language until you've taught it to someone else. We're incarnational creatures, you and me; for truth to be true, it must take on flesh and blood.

The risen Lord tastes of bread and wine!

It's swimming-lesson time. You know she won't drown. She knows she won't drown. But you open the car door and say, "Get in, honey, it's time to go to swimming lessons."

"I'm not going! I'll drown; then you'll be sorry!"

You drag her to the pool. She gets into the water, blows bubbles, goes all the way under, sinks like a rock. She comes up spraying and sputtering, looking at Daddy like he's a serial killer.

A week later, there she is, a three-and-a-half-foot little girl about to jump into the five-foot-deep water with her six-foot daddy looking up at her saying, "It's all right, honey, I'll be right here." Splash!

Next day, 5:15 A.M., she's jumping up and down on your bed: "Is the pool open yet, daddy? Is the pool open yet?"

You see, it wasn't that she didn't know; it was that she didn't *know*.

His name is Ben. All he can do is smile—can't move, can't talk—he just looks at you and smiles. Ben is the son of a physician who lives in the Midwest. Ben suffered an accident when he was two years old. He pulled a cabinet over onto himself, crushing part of his spine. It wasn't anybody's fault. It was an accident.

A friend of mine was the pastor at the church where this physician and his wife were members—good folk, faithful and committed Christians. The first time my friend met Ben was at a dinner party, when the physician came in carrying his sixteen-year-old son in his arms like a sack of potatoes. He looked at the new minister and said, "I don't think you've met our son. This is Ben." The doctor and his wife had struggled for years with grief and guilt about Ben's brokenness.

As a part of a Bible study he was teaching on the Gospel of John, my friend was working with the ninth chapter, the story of the healing of a blind man. It's a little drama, actually, in six scenes, and so my friend, wanting the group to experience the story as a drama, assigned different characters in the story to different members of the study group.

The part of Jesus was read by the physician. He got to the part in the story when the disciples, looking down at the blind beggar, ask Jesus, "Lord, who sinned that this man should have been born blind—he or his parents?" The doctor looked at the words he was to read, and, recognizing in them more of his own pain than he could handle, broke down and started to weep uncontrollably. Everyone sat silent.

After a while, he regained his composure, cleared his throat, and read, "Lord, who sinned that this man should be born blind—he or his parents?"

And then, that Christian doctor read the words of grace from Jesus to his disciples: "Neither he nor his parents, but that the works of God might be manifest in him!" And as he read those words, the grace of God dripped off of him with a healing and a forgiveness and a grace that flooded that room. Choking back the tears, he swallowed hard, and read the words again: "Neither he nor his parents, but that the works of God might be manifest in him!"

He finished reading and sat down. No one said a word. No one had to. For in the word of grace spoken to a blind man, long ago and far away, this physician had heard the word of grace spoken to him.

"Neither he nor his parents, but that the works of God might be manifest in him!"

It wasn't that he didn't know; it was that he didn't *know*. Somehow, holding the book, reading the words, sharing the guilt and the grief, he was finally able to experience the grace.

We're incarnational creatures, you and me. "And when he took bread, and blessed it and broke it and gave it to them, suddenly, they knew!" "It's Jesus!"

And then, he was gone—"vanished from their sight," Luke says. And they were alone again, sitting at the table. But, as strange as it may sound, though they were alone, they weren't *alone* anymore.

I was sitting there "at table" alone, smiling to myself, eating spaghetti, thinking about another time when I was sitting at another table eating spaghetti—or was it bread and wine? I don't know.

But suddenly, I had this feeling: I wasn't really alone!

Has that ever happened to you?

For Further Discussion

1. Why did so many holy sites come to be located on Mount Zion?
2. Given the geography of Jerusalem, why did David choose Jerusalem as the site on which to place his capital?
3. Do you think that Jesus and his disciples were associated with the Essenes?
4. Why has Jesus' last supper with his disciples come to have such religious significance for Christians, both Catholic and Protestant?
5. Do you sense a "presence" when you take Communion? Why is it that so many people do? What do you think is happening there?

NOTES

1. A *gay* is a dramatic, precipitous gorge or valley, as opposed to a broad, level valley or plain, which is called in Hebrew *emek* or *shephelah.*

2. From the Latin *dormitus,* meaning “sleep” (cf. “dormant,” sleeping; “dormitory,” a sleeping place), a euphemism for death. The Roman church commemorates this as the traditional site where Mary died (slept) and, according to the tradition, was taken to heaven.

3. I employ the word “traditional” because almost no scholar believes that the Tomb of David is located on modern Mount Zion. The present site is the result of early Christian identification of the City of David with the southwestern peak of the Old City, present-day Mount Zion, owing to the fact that 1 Kings 2:10 states that David was buried in the City of David. In their day, as today, the southwestern peak was indeed known as Sion (Zion in Greek). However, it was not so in David’s time. Rather, David’s Sion was located on the City of David, or Hill Ophel (in Silwan), and almost certainly David was buried there, not on modern Mount Zion.

4. The Latin word *cenaculum* also means “dining room,” which typically was an upper-story room. See Jack Finegan, *The Archeology of the New Testament: The Life of Jesus and the Beginning of the Early Church* (Princeton, N.J.: Princeton University Press, 1978), 147.

5. The famous Madaba Mosaic Map (a mosaic map of Jerusalem found in Madaba, Jordan, and dating from around 560 CE), locates a church known at the time as the Sancta Sion (Holy Sion) on this site, and identifies the church as the location of the upper room. When you enter the Church of the Dormition today, you will notice above the portal the words “Sancta Sion.”

6. The sermon that follows was first published in *Pulpit Digest* 75, no. 528 (July/August 1994): 48–52. Reprinted by permission.

CHAPTER 11

The Church of the Holy Sepulchre

There is virtually universal agreement among New Testament archaeologists that the murky, medieval medley of buildings called the Church of the Holy Sepulchre (tomb) sits atop what was once the place of Golgotha and the tomb of Jesus. That the earliest Christians would have venerated the site is indisputable, and the memory to which that veneration bore witness, despite the centuries of Jerusalem's upheaval, most likely would have persevered.

The tradition of the veneration of the site now occupied by the Church of the Holy Sepulchre is early and substantial. Jerome of Bethlehem, translator of the Latin Vulgate, wrote in his *Letter 58 to Paulinus* (395) that from the reign of Emperor Hadrian (second century) to that of Emperor Constantine (fourth century), the place of Jesus' resurrection had been occupied by a statue of Jupiter (Zeus in Greek), and that the rock escarpment on which Jesus' cross had stood bore a statue of Venus (Aphrodite in Greek). In this way, Jerome explains, the Romans "supposed that by polluting our holy places they would deprive us of our faith in the passion and the resurrection."[1] Likewise, the early Christian historian Eusebius (d. 340) wrote that Hadrian covered with earth the tomb in which Jesus had been buried and paved the entire area, there erecting a shrine to the goddess Venus, apparently as a part of his systematic profanation of Jewish and Christian holy places, which he conducted in the wake of the Third Jewish Revolt (132–135).[2] Moreover, Eusebius, in his *Life of Constantine,* reports that Emperor Constantine, upon his conversion to Christianity, ordered the removal of the statue of Venus, and that while this was being done, "contrary to all expectation" a tomb was revealed, which was taken to be the very tomb in which Christ had been buried and from which he was raised from the dead.[3] Eusebius notes elsewhere that the place of Jesus' resurrection was near the place of his crucifixion, "the place of a skull," he calls it.[4] In the fourth century, an unidentified pilgrim to the Holy Land known as the Pilgrim of Bordeaux described the proximity of the tomb to the place of crucifixion as being "about a stone's throw" away.[5] Upon discovery of the holy site, Constantine immediately ordered a church to be constructed there, and the church, called the Church of the Anastasis (Church of the Resurrection), was dedicated in 335. The church, however, was not completed until 384 so that workmen could cut away the rock face of the cliff from around the tomb to isolate the tomb from the surrounding rock. It is for this reason that pilgrims to the Church of the Holy Sepulchre today are disappointed not to encounter the rocky escarpment referred to in the New Testament as Golgotha, the "skull hill" that long ago was chipped away to make room for the present church.

At this point it should be noted that the objection to the authenticity of the site—the location of the Church of the Holy Sepulchre is inside the wall of the city rather than outside, as the New Testament describes the place of Jesus' crucifixion (cf. Hebrews 13:12)—is ameliorated by the fact that the present wall of the Old City of Jerusalem (its third) is not the wall that was present in Jesus' time. The church was outside that wall and lay in an area of an old quarry that had been utilized as a cemetery.[6]

The church that Constantine built was comprised of four basic elements: an atrium; a covered basilica; an open courtyard, which contained the block of stone thought to be the residual rock of Golgotha; and a rotunda housing the tomb itself.[7] This church, however, would undergo several restorations and reconstructions in its long history. The first occurred in the seventh century when the Persians set the church on fire, necessitating its restoration, which was undertaken by the patriarch Modestus. This restoration made no significant changes in the church Constantine had built. However, the edifice would not fare so well in the eleventh century. The Moslem caliph Fatamide systematically destroyed the entire complex in 1009, even having his workmen take picks and hammers to the rock tomb housed in the rotunda. It was not until the eleventh century that a reconstruction of the church was undertaken, but the devastation was so complete, and the funds so inadequate, that much of Constantine's church had to be abandoned. Only the courtyard and the rotunda were rebuilt; the outer two elements of the church, the atrium and the basilica, were lost forever. Today, those two areas are occupied by an open-air promenade leading up to the entrance to what was the courtyard in Constantine's church. The final alteration was undertaken in the twelfth century when the Crusaders covered the courtyard with a Romanesque church adjoined to the eleventh-century restored rotunda. It is this building that pilgrims enter today. Nothing of the original fourth-century Constantinian Church of the Anastasis remains.

I've never liked the Church of the Holy Sepulchre. It just seems so inappropriate. It is the central shrine of the Christian faith. It houses the place where the two most significant events for the Christian church occurred, the crucifixion and the resurrection. And yet, I guess I expected more. Jerome Murphy-O'Connor writes of it,

> One expects the central shrine of Christendom to stand out in majestic isolation, but anonymous buildings cling to it like barnacles. One looks for numinous light, but it is dark and cramped. One hopes for peace, but the ear is assailed by a cacophony of warring chants. One desires holiness, only to encounter a jealous possessiveness: the six groups of occupants—Latin Catholics, Greek Orthodox, Armenians, Syrians, Copts, Ethiopians—watch one another suspiciously for any infringement of right. The frailty of man is nowhere more apparent than here; it epitomizes the human condition.[8]

Noisy, busy, jostling, dark, dank—it just doesn't seem right somehow that this should be the place so central to my faith. I much prefer the Garden Tomb—quiet, peaceful, reflective, bright, airy. That's more like it. Or the Mount of Olives—olive groves, gardens, sloping hillsides, beautiful vistas. One can believe in the mystic and majestic in such places. It's no wonder, then, that the crowd erupted into jubilant shouts of "Hosanna!" when Jesus crested the Mount of Olives on that first Palm Sunday. I'll bet there would have been no hosannas shouted had Jesus made his entrance into Jerusalem at the Church of the Holy Sepulchre.

But then again, the church has always preferred palms to passion, gardens to tombs, Olivet to Golgotha. And yet, nowhere is the juxtaposition that is so central to the gospel displayed more compellingly than in this noisy, bustling, dark, dank "tomb" of a church. Maybe that's why a week that began as coronation ended with crucifixion. For Jesus was indeed destined to wear a crown, a "death crown."

The Scripture: Isaiah 50:4–6

The Lord God has given me
the tongue of those who are taught,
that I may know how to sustain with a word
him that is weary.
Morning by morning he wakens,
he wakens my ear
to hear as those who are taught.
The Lord God has opened my ear,
and I was not rebellious,
I turned not backward.
I gave my back to the smiters,
and my cheeks to those who pulled out the beard;
I hid not my face
from shame and spitting. (RSV)

"Death Crown"

In a moving short story called "Death Crown," North Carolinian Robert Morgan writes about a woman from the mountains of western North Carolina who comes to stay with her great aunt, who is in the last hours of life.[9] The woman's name is Ellen, and her great aunt Alice, her mother's aunt, had always been her favorite relative, although the bond between them was strange indeed. You see, when Alice was a little girl, she contracted what mountain people called "the white swelling," a severe inflammation around an open wound. It frequently caused a very high fever, and sometimes, even death. Back in those days, before penicillin and other antibiotics, infections of this kind ran without check; and when Alice was accidentally kicked by an animal while in the barnyard, the resulting laceration quickly went into the white swelling.

Alice recovered physically, but the weeks of fever stopped her mental development in its tracks. She never progressed intellectually much beyond a second or third grader. In time, she grew into a beautiful young woman, but her mind remained that of a little girl. As a result, she became the "family embarrassment." People in the neighborhood saw this grown-up woman with a child's mind and couldn't understand. And what they couldn't understand frightened them. Some people said she was crazy; others said she was possessed. But Alice wasn't evil, just simple, and her simplicity and innocence threatened people, frightened people—except for Ellen. Whenever Ellen's family would go to visit Alice, Ellen took her a little gift, some candy or a doll to play with. And Ellen and Alice played together like sisters, even though this woman was old enough to be her grandmother.

Every time Ellen went to her grandmother's house to visit, she spent all her time with Alice. They played hopscotch together; they ran in the meadow together; they rolled in the grass together like best friends—this old, white-haired woman and the little girl. Alice never showed any malice or ill will toward anyone. If there was ever a pure, saintly woman, it was Ellen's aunt Alice.

And now, in her eighties, she was dying, and Ellen had come to sit there by the bed with her so she'd know she was not alone. Sitting there with this little old woman she had loved so much, but who was perpetually trapped in childhood, Ellen stared down at her and thought to herself,

> The way her head sinks into the pillow kind of reminds me of the old story of the death crown. Old-timers used to say that when a really good person is sick for a long time before they die, that the feathers in the pillow will knit themselves into a crown that fits the person's head. The crown won't be found till after they are dead, of course, but it's a certain sign of another crown in heaven, my daddy used to say. I've never seen one myself but the old-timers say they're woven so tight they never come apart and they shine like gold even though they're so light they might just as well be a ring of light.[10]

A "death crown" visible only on the other side of death, turning what was, only a moment before, an ultimate defeat into a triumphant victory. "Death . . . crown." Do you get the irony, the paradox of that? In literature we call this kind of figure of speech an oxymoron, putting two words together that don't seem to belong together, like "jumbo shrimp." It's an oxymoron. "Death crown." Get it? What an amazing transformation of images!

It's a transformation that, I think, the anonymous composer of the so-called third Servant Song of Isaiah (Isaiah 50:4–9) would have understood. There, the writer describes the ultimate vindication and redemption of the humiliated Suffering Servant despite the fickle faithlessness of Israel's rejection of him:

> For the Lord God helps me;
> therefore I have not been confounded;
> therefore I have set my face like a flint,
> and I know that I shall not be put to shame;
> he who vindicates me is near. (Isaiah 50:7–8a, RSV)

And centuries later, the church, reflecting on the events that had transpired in the place they had come to venerate as the Church of the Holy Sepulchre (note the irony of *Holy* Sepulchre), reached back to that image and to those words to try to understand what had gone so terribly wrong between Olivet and Golgotha, between Palm Sunday and Good Friday, between coronation and crucifixion. And then they knew: Jesus, like Isaiah's Servant before him, was indeed to receive a crown, a death crown. "And he set his face," Luke would write, "to go to Jerusalem" (Luke 9:51).

Oh, don't get me wrong. It's great fun to wave the palms and shout "Hosanna! Blessed is the one who comes in the name of the Lord" with all the others who welcomed Jesus through the Eastern Gate on that Palm Sunday long ago. But by the end of the week that same crowd was shouting "Crucify him! Crucify him!" And throughout the centuries the church has somehow almost instinctively understood that Palm Sunday is too soon to crown him Messiah. Not here. Not yet. Not on Olivet. Not on that side of the cross.

I find it interesting that not a single New Testament writer develops theologically the triumphal entry of Jesus. Not one. Not Paul, not Peter, not John, not the writer of Hebrews—none of the great New Testament theologians does a thing with it. When Paul, the greatest New Testament theologian, developed his theology of pastoral care for the churches he'd established, it would be passion not palms to which he would turn. And it's not that New Testament people didn't know anything of Jesus' life save his crucifixion and resurrection. Other major events in Jesus' life receive theological development: his birth, his agony in the garden of Gethsemane, even his transfiguration. But when it comes to his triumphal entry, not a word. Why? Because the crowd waving palms and shouting hosannas on that side of the cross was wrong. His crown was to be a death crown.

Don't get me wrong. Christianity is a thing of great joy and great comfort. But Christianity does not begin in joy and comfort; it begins in pain and suffering and death:

> I gave my back to those who smite,
> I gave my cheeks to those who pulled out the beard;
> I gave my face to those who spit;
> and I gave my ear to God and he opened my ear,
> dug out my ear, to hear as those who are taught.
> (Isaiah 50:6, 4b, my translation)

And therein is our hope. Without the cross our faith wouldn't be a comfort to anybody. What would you say to the terminal cancer victim? What would you say to the mother who just buried her baby gunned down on the mean streets of Kosovo or New Orleans or Miami? What do you say to the eighty-five-year-old man, alone and forgotten, in cold storage in some nursing home with no one to care? "Smile, God loves you!" No.

But I'll tell you what you can say. You can say that you believe in a God who's been there before you, in the pain, in the darkness, in the loneliness, in the death, and in a Christ who has come through it all and who lives and reigns now on the far side of the cross. And you can say that you believe in a church that is willing to take up its own cross and the crosses of those whom the world crucifies daily. Jesus is rarely to be found among the "successful," at least as the world defines success. He wears a crown, all right, but it's a death crown!

And you can be sure of this, too: wherever a cross is raised in our world, Christ will be there with the crucified, not the crucifiers. And if we're his people, we'll be there too, proclaiming the presence of the crucified God.

William Willimon, dean of the chapel at Duke University, tells about a Communion service at which he presided one Sunday at the chapel.[11] Before serving the Communion elements, Willimon's pattern was to raise his hands in a cruciform gesture and offer a prayer of thanksgiving for the bread and cup that the congregation was about to receive. On this Sunday, however, when he raised his hands to bless the bread and cup, a little girl sitting next to her mother noticed for the first time what Willimon was doing, and leaned over and whispered to her mother, "Look, Mommy, he's trying to look like Jesus on the cross!" Muted snickers rippled through the congregation.

But you know what? It occurs to me that that's not a bad thing to say about a Christian. Is it.

For Further Discussion

1. Why did early Christians in the Holy Land choose to preserve sacred sites by building churches on them rather than by preserving them unchanged?

2. How does it make you feel to know that six different Christian groups compete for the holiest site in the Holy Land? How do you think it makes God feel?

3. In what ways is the Church of the Holy Sepulchre in Jerusalem well suited as the place that commemorates the crucifixion of Jesus?

4. Why did New Testament Christians never develop theologically the imagery of Jesus' triumphal entry in their thinking about Christ?

5. Discuss the irony of the idea of a crucified Messiah and Christ's death crown.

NOTES

1. Jack Finegan, *The Archeology of the New Testament: The Life of Jesus and the Beginning of the Early Church* (Princeton, N.J.: Princeton University Press, 1978), 22–23.

2. Ibid., 164.

3. Ibid.

4. Ibid.

5. Ibid.

6. Ibid.

7. Jerome Murphy-O'Connor, *The Holy Land: An Archaeological Guide from Earliest Times to 1700,* rev. ed. (New York: Oxford University Press, 1986), 45.

8. Ibid., 43.

9. Robert Morgan, "Death Crown," in *New Stories from the South: The Year's Best, 1992,* ed. Shannon Ravenel (Chapel Hill, N.C.: Algonquin Books of Chapel Hill, 1992), 85–102.

10. Ibid., 95.

11. William H. Willimon, *Sunday Dinner: The Lord's Supper and the Christian Life* (Nashville: The Upper Room, 1981), 90.

CHAPTER 12

The Pool of Bethesda

Just inside St. Stephen's Gate on the northeastern side of the Old City, in the Muslim Quarter, lie the beautiful gardens and medieval cloister of the White Fathers, a North African Roman Catholic order known for its all-white habits, to whom the Pool of Bethesda and the Church of St. Anne were entrusted after the

Ottomans delivered the site to Napoleon in 1856 in gratitude for his assistance in the Crimean War.[1] Though today the site is situated just inside the walls of the Old City, in the time of Jesus it lay just outside the northern wall of the city, about six hundred yards east of the Antonia, the citadel built by Herod the Great on the northwest corner of the temple and named for his friend and patron, Marc Antony.

The site of the pool lay buried beneath debris for centuries until excavated in the 1960s by the White Fathers. Their excavations have largely vindicated the account in John 5 of the existence on the site of a pool, which John called Bethesda, the "House of the Two Pools."

Intriguingly, John's description of the site is quite specific: "Now there is in Jerusalem, by the sheep gate [market], a pool called in Hebrew Bethesda, which has five porches." That's a little like saying, "On the corner, next to the post office, there's a MacDonald's." Presumably, anyone living in Jerusalem at the time would have known immediately the place of which John was speaking. The problem is that no other ancient writer ever mentions such a pool, and no such five-sided building—which would seem to be demanded to meet John's description—is referenced in any writing from antiquity. John's credibility was suspect. And yet, his description is so specific that he seems to assume that everyone reading his Gospel would know exactly the pool to which he referred. Now, we know they would have.

John's mention of the sheep gate is precise. Actually, the Greek says, "Now there is in Jerusalem, near the sheep, a pool." The word John uses is *probatikē* (dative case for the word "belonging to sheep"), here used as a substantival adjective, literally, "at the sheep place." Presumably, anyone from Jerusalem would have known what "at the sheep place" meant. A reasonable hypothesis is that the reference was either to a sheep *gate* (so RSV), or to a sheep *market* (so KJV). More likely, however, is that both were intended: a gate leading outside the city, just beyond which lay a sheep market, would have come to be known as the "sheep gate." Locals tell me that up until recently (within the last fifty or so years), there has been a sheep market in the area. Indeed, a sheep gate was mentioned by Nehemiah (3:1; 12:39), which, from the descriptions given in the passages, seems to have been situated on the north city wall just outside the temple area, the very location John described.

The pool near the sheep gate John called Bethesda. In Hebrew, Bethesda means "house/place of pouring," and so, by extension, of a "pool." The existence of a pool called Bethesda in the city of Jerusalem at the time of Jesus has now been confirmed by the Dead Sea Scrolls. In the famous Copper Scroll from Qumran (3Q15), written probably sometime prior to 68 CE, a list of places in Jerusalem is cited. Among them is this one: "At Bethesda [*Beth Eshdathayin*], in the pool where you enter its small[er] reservoir . . ." (11:12–13).[2] What is even more striking about the Copper Scroll's reference to Bethesda is its spelling: it uses a Hebrew dual form *(ayin)*. Note also that the scroll describes the pool as having a "smaller" reservoir, which, one presumes, indicates the presence of a larger one. Hence, the Dead Sea Scrolls attest to a pool in Jerusalem known at the time as Bethesda, the "House of the Two Pools."[3]

Twin pools surrounded by covered porches *(stoas)* were precisely what the White Fathers found in their excavations in the 1960s: two pools rectangular in shape, a larger pool to the south and a smaller to the north, separated by a dike of stone nearly twenty feet in width. The pools were situated in a small valley, now filled in, that ran diagonally to the Kidron Valley. No doubt, the pools were thus placed to act as reservoirs, just as the Copper Scroll described, to collect runoff rainwater on its way to the Kidron. The pools may have also been supplied by a spring that intermittently bubbled to the surface, thus accounting for the legend of the angel who troubled the waters, to which some manuscripts of John refer (John 5:4). Excavations have revealed numerous columns, capitals, and bases indicating that the pools were surrounded by five colonnaded porticoes (one each around the perimeter of the pools and one on the dike through the middle), just as John described.

Originally constructed by the high priest Simon in the second century BCE to supply water for the temple, the pools were replaced in the first century BCE by Herod the Great, who dug the Pool of Israel much closer to the temple.[4] Early on, the pools came to be associated with miraculous healings. Excavations revealed that in the second century an Asclepian occupied the site. Asclepius (also known as Serapis), the Greek god of healing, was venerated in several sites in the ancient world, perhaps the most famous being Pergamum. His devotees typically gathered in shrines known as Asclepians, where hot springs or other sources of water fed ritual baths in which the afflicted immersed themselves, hoping for healing. That Asclepius was worshiped at the site confirms its early association with healing.

In the Byzantine period (324–680 CE), Roman Christians destroyed the pagan Asclepian and erected a church on the site. The church seems to have carried twin associations: both the healing of the lame man in John 5, and the birthplace of Mary, the mother of Jesus.[5] The church was destroyed by the Persians in 614, and a small chapel was erected on the site by Jerusalem Christians sometime afterward.[6] When the Crusaders arrived in 1099, the little chapel was in ruins. They constructed a new Romanesque basilica on the site and dedicated it to St. Anne, the mother of Mary, according to early Christian tradition. When Saladin drove out the Crusaders in 1192, he converted the chapel into a Muslim school, and it remained so until given to Napoleon in 1856. In 1878 the chapel became the property of the White Fathers, who undertook excavations on the site. The Church of St. Anne one sees today is that same chapel, but restored and enlarged. It commemorates the traditional site of the home of Anne and Joachim, parents of Mary, the mother of Jesus. According to tradition, Joachim was a shepherd, and so the association with the sheep market in the area was a natural one.

Of course, it's just tradition, but if the site is in any way genuine, I can imagine that Jesus on more than one occasion visited in the home of his grandparents, Anne and Joachim, who lived right next door to the pool. If so, it would account for an intriguing comment John makes in his description of Jesus' healing of the lame man who for thirty-eight years had been lying by the pool in the hope that when the angel troubled the waters, he'd be the first one in and thus would be healed. John remarks rather casually, "Jesus knew that he had been lying there for a long time." How could Jesus have known that he'd been lying there for a long time? Perhaps because when he visited his maternal grandparents—who lived right next door to the pool—at "Thanksgiving," he'd seen that pathetic old man lying there year after year, hoping against hope that the impossible would happen and he would be healed. And I can just imagine that the young Jesus, witnessing that little drama, took note of that man (I remind you that Jesus never missed a thing—he once noticed a fallen sparrow!), and said to himself, "You know, one day I'm gonna do something about that." And one day, he did.

The Scripture: John 5:2–16

Now there is in Jerusalem near the Sheep Gate a pool, called in Hebrew Bethesda, which has five porches. At these lay a multitude of sick, blind, lame, and those with withered limbs. There was a man there who for thirty-eight years had been ill. Jesus, having seen this one lying [there], and knowing that he had been there for a long time, said to him, "Do you wish to be made whole?" The sick man answered, "Sir, I have no one who, when the water is troubled, will put me in the pool, and when I go, another goes down before me." Jesus said to him, "Arise, take up your pallet and walk." And immediately the man became well and took up his pallet and walked.

Now it was the sabbath day. Therefore, the Jews were saying to the healed man, "It is the sabbath, and it is unlawful for you to carry your pallet [on the sabbath]." And he answered them, "The one who made me well, that one said to me, 'Take up your pallet and walk.'" They asked him, "Who is the man who said to you, 'Take your pallet and walk'?" But the man who had been healed did not know who he was, for Jesus had slipped away, there being a crowd in the place. Afterwards, Jesus found him in the temple and said to him, "Behold, you have become well; sin no longer, lest a worse [thing] overtake you." The man departed and told the Jews that Jesus was the one who made him well. And because of this the Jews persecuted Jesus, because he did these things on the sabbath.

"A Cruel Pool"

What a beautiful story. What a wonderful dream. Waters that not only cleanse, but also heal. Healing waters. A purifying pool.

The third sign in John's story takes place by such a pool of promise. Bethesda was its name. It had originally been a part of Herod the Great's water retention system, situated on the northeast corner of the temple mount. All the water running down the small valley on the north side of the temple toward the Kidron would collect in this colonnaded pool for use in the temple. But better sources of water were devised, and Bethesda was no longer needed for temple water. Nevertheless, it continued in use, right up to Jesus' day. It became a place where worshipers, on their way to the temple to offer sacrifices, could stop and wash their animals before entering the temple with them—a "sheep dip," a *mikvah* for sacrifices, if you will, in which animals were rather unceremoniously dunked in ritual purification.

And as time went by, a legend began to develop around this pool—"Did you hear what happened to Simeon ben Yeshua at Bethesda yesterday?"—a legend, later elaborated, that said that periodically, when conditions were just right, an angel would come down from heaven and miraculously stir the waters of the pool, and the first one into the water after that would be healed. And so, on their way to work in the morning, they'd drop off their sick relatives there by the pool with a Pepsi and a package of cheese crackers and say, "Now, if you're not healed, I'll pick you up tonight on my way home from work."

What an indictment of the temple that must have been! Right outside the walls of the city, a stone's throw away from God's house, a host of unwashed, disaffected incorrigibles gather at the pool to find what little hope can be had in their miserable lives—hope, they've come to believe, that can't be found in the house of God just on the other side of the wall.

"We've been missing you at church lately."

"Well, we're at the pool now. We go to the pool; that's where it's really happening!"

And what's going on at the pool? There they were, the desperate wretched lying there with their faces turned toward the water, waiting for the pool to be stirred. From time to time, the wind would lap on the surface of the water, and they'd go rolling off down into the water, and out they'd come wheezing, coughing, and chilled to the bone: "Must have been the wind." And if the angel did stir the water, who do you think would be the first one in? Those who were all bent over and diseased and really crippled? No, no, no. Of course not. Those with chapped lips or a hangnail or something like that, that's who. No, the pool's no better than the temple. It's a cruel pool. It does not heal the sick; it taunts them. The whole fly-swarming, foul-smelling scene is a judgment on the kind of religion that has everything to offer those who don't really need it and nothing for those who do.[7]

And Jesus comes to the man who has been lying there for thirty-eight years and says to him, "Do you wish to be made whole?" The Greek could also be rendered "Are you willing to become well?" The word translated "well" *(hygiēs)* gives us our English word "hygiene." It's a health term. It can be used for physical health or for health in the larger sense.

And the man said, "I have no one to put me into the water. . . ."

"Rise, take up your pallet and walk!" exclaims Jesus. And for the first time in thirty-eight years the man walks! He picks up his pallet and gleefully goes bounding down the street.

But there's a complicating factor in the story. It's the sabbath day, and as the man is bounding down the street, suddenly he's stopped.

"You're under arrest!"

"What?"

"You heard me. You're under arrest! It's the sabbath and you're carrying your pallet. The law says, 'Six days shall you work, but on the sabbath you shall not work.'"

"But Jesus told me to. . . ."

"I don't care what Jesus said; the Bible says. . . ."

"But Jesus says. . . ."

"The Bible says. . . ."

This wasn't the first time, or the last, when people of faith would have to choose between Jesus and the Bible.

And can you beat that! Thirty-eight years the poor guy's been lying there, waiting to be healed, and suddenly he's healed on the wrong day! It's a comedy of errors. But nonetheless, Jesus did heal him, and so that for the first time in thirty-eight years he was able to stand up and walk on his own.

Then, later, Jesus found the man and dealt with him on another level. He dealt with him where he was crippled within by sin, by guilt. "Look," Jesus said, "you have become whole, well; continue no longer in sin, lest a worse thing happen to you."

But the healing creates a problem not only for the crippled man, but also for Jesus. Because Jesus had healed the man on the Sabbath, he offended the piety of those who had an entirely different agenda for religion. The focus of their piety was on the calendar, a day of the week, and this to them was to take priority over what Jesus had just done.

But here, as elsewhere, the focus of Jesus' piety was quite different. The focus of his piety was on a human being and his needs, and in this case the needs were multiple. The priority of Jesus' mission was to find a human being in need—whether conscious of the need or not—and to minister to that person at whatever level of need there might be.

So here, two pieties met, two religions really—superficially, all the same religion. Both Jesus and his critics would have been known as Jews, followers of a Jewish faith. But within that same Judaism were two entirely different agendas. On the one hand, there was a piety that gave priority to a religious calendar over the needs of a person, and on the other hand, there was the piety of Jesus, who was no iconoclast out to smash religious custom just for the sake of doing it. The Gospels plainly tell us that it was Jesus' custom on the Sabbath to go to the synagogue, the recognized place of worship, and there engage with others in worship. On occasion, Jesus did fast; he observed various calendar days. It was not that he was against these things as such, but that he had priorities that took precedence over any one of these things. Furthermore, whenever there was a choice between a human being and his or her needs—whether physical, emotional, volitional (the way one exercises one's options), or relational (how one relates to God, to other people, to one's self, or to things)—there was never any question about the priorities of Jesus. His priorities were personal; they were not things, not even religious things, like the Sabbath day or a rite of fasting or a rite of a particular day of worship.

Later on, in the seventh chapter of John, this same story is echoed. What Jesus had done for this man on the Sabbath had rankled the piety of those who quarreled with Jesus. The controversy is still simmering when Jesus turns to face his critics: "You accuse me of violating the law of Moses. Well, didn't Moses also command that you circumcise on the eighth day? But if the eighth day falls on the sabbath, I notice that you circumcise on the sabbath, despite the prohibition against doing anything on the sabbath. Well, if you do that, are you angry with me because I made a whole man well on the sabbath?" (John 7:19–23, my paraphrase).

But what catches my attention in this story are the questions Jesus asks. Listen to his questions.[8]

The first one is a strange one, is it not? Jesus says to this man who for thirty-eight years had been crippled, "Do you wish to become well?" What a strange question for a man like that. What did he expect him to say? "No, in thirty-eight years the thought's never entered my mind." He had been at that pool in the belief that the first one in would get healed. Every indication is that he really wanted to be healed.

And yet, it is a proper question to put to one who is crippled or to one who is ill or to one who suffers any kind of impairment. "Do you wish to become well?" You see, not all sick people want to become well. There are some advantages to not being well. We escape certain responsibilities and receive attention and all of that. It is not just that we are diseased; it is that we are addicted to our disease.

I knew a lady in a church I pastored who simply did not understand that when people ask you how you're doing, they're just being polite; they don't really want to know. But she'd tell you, and tell you, and tell you. If you asked her husband how she was doing, he'd say, "Oh, she's not doing very well. But don't be too concerned, she's enjoyed ill-health for years."

So, it is a proper question, and yet we must immediately sound a disclaimer, because there is that atrocious theology that says, "If you're sick, you really don't want to be well." Or, "If you're sick, you deserve to be sick." Or, "If you're sick, God wills that you be sick." That's the meanest theology I know, and Jesus rejected it, straight out.

Do you remember in John 9 what Jesus said to the disciples when they inquired about the condition of a blind man? "Lord," they asked, "who sinned that this man should be born blind, he or his parents?" Do you hear the theology being expressed by the disciples? Illness, misfortune, or disability is the result of the judgment of God. And Jesus said, "Neither. This man is blind so that the glory of God might be manifest in him."

So, in no sense are we to get from this story the idea that all sick people, all people with impairment, want it that way or deserve to have it that way, or that they are necessarily lacking in piety or faith or prayer. Some of the finest people we know, people of piety and faith and prayer, are people who have never known a day without pain.

But it is a proper question, isn't it. "Do you wish to be well?" In this man's case, at least, it was a factor. Some matters are involuntary; there's not a thing we can do about them. But some matters are voluntary; we do have a say in the situation or the outcome. And our responsibility is not for the involuntary factors that affect whether or not we are well; our responsibility is for the voluntary factors, where we do have a say.

But there's another question in this story. In John 7:23, Jesus puts this question to his accusers: "Are you angry with me, you religionists, you who are hung up on this and that and on what you call piety, are you angry with me because I made a whole man whole on the sabbath?"

Now, when Jesus says, "I made a whole man whole on the sabbath," there's a play on words in the Greek. I've tried to retain it in my translation. The first word is just our word "whole," meaning "complete" or "total." And so, it was the "total" man, both physical and spiritual, whom Jesus healed that day. But the second word is the same word John used for "well" in 5:6. It's the word from which we get "hygiene" in English. It's a health term.

Do you get the pun? "I made a whole man whole." I made the "total" man "healthy."

There are different ways of perceiving salvation. It can be perceived as conversion: you go in one way, turn around, and go out the other way. It can be perceived as a death, burial, and resurrection, the end of an old kind of life and the beginning of a new. There are any number of ways in which to portray salvation, and what God has done for us in Jesus Christ. But don't miss this one: salvation, the salvation that Jesus Christ came to offer is the offer of health, wholeness, healing. He is on the side of health for the body; he is on the side of health for the feelings, for the emotions; for the exercise of our awesome power of choice, what we mistakenly call will power, where we can choose, where we can say yes or no not only to the ordinary options of life, but yes or no even to God, our Maker. That's the awesome freedom and the awesome responsibility that belong to being human.

You see, we humans are created in the image of God in the hope that we will achieve our true humanity, realized for us in Jesus Christ, who is our true human destiny. As Paul puts it, "For those whom he foreknew he also predestined [that we be] conformed to the image of his Son, to the end that he should be the firstborn of many brothers and sisters" (Romans 8:29). But most of us deny that destiny in one of two ways: we either arrogantly aspire to be more than fully human, or we apathetically acquiesce to being less than fully human. Either is a denial of the good thing God created us to be: fully human—nothing more, nothing less, nothing other.

We are creatures created in the image of God. We are creatures; we are not angels. Some misguided theologies teach that we'll all become angels when we die. It would be a total loss if we were ever to become angels, in this life or the next! God didn't create us to be angels. God's got angels to be angels, and doesn't need us to become angels. God created us to be humans, not angels.

But neither are we mere brutes, animals, merely responding to instinct. To be sure, we are creatures, but we are not just creatures; we are creatures created in God's image. Indeed, there is a sense in which none of us ever fully realizes our true potential to be a human being, with all that that means, unless and until we find the fulfillment of our humanity in Christ. Apart from that, we're not fully human. We're something less than fully human—brutish, barbarian, beastly, but not human—never having achieved our true destiny of being "creatures created in the image of God."

And so, what is salvation? From one perspective, the perspective of this story, it is God's work in Jesus Christ offering to us, if we will receive it, wholeness, health, so that the total person is brought on the way to true personhood: to become, in relationship with God, fully human—nothing more, nothing less, and nothing other. And isn't that what you want? I mean, what you *really* want?

It's a beautiful dream. Miracle waters. A pool of promise. But alas, Bethesda is a cruel place; the miracle turns out to be only for the few, the enterprising, and the early. The pool cannot deliver what it promises, for what you want, what you really want, can't be found in a pool. It can only be found in a person.

And so, look up! Standing by the water is a stranger who is fulfilling its promise. Listen! He's asking a question; he's making an offer.

And I wonder. What will you do? Well?

For Further Discussion

1. Why do scholars regard the Pool of Bethesda to be one of the most authentic sites in the Holy Land?
2. Why would ancient peoples regard a pool as having healing properties?
3. Why did Jesus ask the lame man if he wanted to be healed?
4. In what ways is the concept of health an appropriate one for the Christian understanding of salvation?
5. What does it mean to be fully human?
6. To what extent have people today, having been disillusioned with organized religion, turned to twenty-first century versions of "the pool" to find what they really seek?

NOTES

1. See Jerome Murphy-O'Connor, *The Holy Land: An Archaeological Guide from Earliest Times to 1700,* rev. ed. (New York: Oxford University Press, 1986), 29–33.

2. Cited in Jack Finegan, *The Archeology of the New Testament: The Life of Jesus and the Beginning of the Early Church* (Princeton, N.J.: Princeton University Press, 1978), 143.

3. So J. T. Milik, "Le rouleau de cuivre provenant de la Grotte 3Q (3Q15)," in *Les 'Petites Grottes' de Qumran,* ed. M. Baillet, J. T. Milik, and R. de Vaux (Oxford: Clarendon Press, 1962), 214, 271.

4. Murphy-O'Connor, *The Holy Land,* 29.

5. Finegan, *Archeology of the New Testament,* 144–47.

6. Ibid., 145.

7. Parts of the description of the scene by the pool are dependent upon a sermon I heard Fred B. Craddock preach on this text, and parts upon his comments on this passage in *John* (Atlanta: John Knox Press, 1982), 43.

8. The interpretation that follows is dependent in large part upon the exegetical and theological wisdom of my beloved teacher and dear friend, Frank Stagg. See his book *The Doctrine of Christ* (Nashville: Convention Press, 1984), 67–76.

CHAPTER 13

Gordon's Calvary

On the north side of the Old City of Jerusalem, nestled beneath a canopy of oaks and pines, is a place well known to Christian pilgrims, who wouldn't think of visiting the Holy Land without a trip to "Gordon's Calvary" and the "Garden Tomb" (see chapter 14). These two sites are located in a much appreciated pastoral oasis in the middle of the desert din of city sights and smells and sounds that assault the senses and exhaust the resolve to focus on the "spiritual."

Gordon's Calvary takes its name from the British general Charles Gordon, who in 1883 visited this site and thought he spied, staring vacuously from the rock cliff, what appeared to be the shape of a human skull. Noting the eye sockets, the bridge of limestone resembling a human nose, and a large cave below in the shape of a mouth agape, Gordon believed that he had discovered the place identified in all four Gospels as Golgotha, the "Place of the Skull," where Jesus was crucified. Whether or not he did is a matter of much dispute, but the skull hill that Gordon discovered is not without claim to authenticity. For example, the skull hill, now, as in the first century, is situated outside the city wall. It is well known that in the first century crucifixions took place outside the city to ameliorate Jewish concerns about defiling with corpses the places where Jewish people lived. Moreover, John, in his Gospel, implies as much when he says, "And seizing his own cross, Jesus *went out* unto what is called the Skull Place, which is called in Hebrew Golgotha" (John 19:17). And the writer of the book of Revelation, in describing the martyrs who follow their Lord even unto death, depicts the martyrdom of the saints as a harvest of grapes in which the blood of the martyrs is squeezed out as one squeezes grapes in a wine press. The writer notes that, as with the death of their Lord, "the wine press was trodden *outside the city*" (Revelation 14:20).

Also in its favor is that Gordon's Calvary was (and still is) situated at the intersection of a busy thoroughfare. The Romans employed other methods of execution far more cost effective and far less time consuming than crucifixion.

Crucifixion was not merely a method of execution; it was a statement. Thus, the Romans typically crucified their victims in very public places, such as the intersections of major thoroughfares, to maximize the impact. The Gospels seem to corroborate this in noting that passersby taunted Jesus and the other victims as they hung in full view of people going into and out of the city. Moreover, John says that "many of the Jews read the title [that Pilate had placed on Jesus' cross], because the place where Jesus was crucified was near the city," and that the title over Jesus was written "in Hebrew, Latin, and Greek," thus making it understandable to all who might pass that way on their way to the city, regardless of what language they spoke (John 19:20). The site of Gordon's Calvary is situated on just such an ancient thoroughfare. Indeed, even today, the terminal for Israel's excellent mass transit bus system, the Egged, is located right next to the skull hill.

Roman Catholics, and most New Testament archaeologists, argue that the Church of the Holy Sepulchre (see chapter 11) has a far greater claim to authenticity than does Gordon's Calvary. Some Roman Catholics contend that General Gordon, a Protestant, was simply trying to identify a holy place that would carry the same spiritual and emotional significance for Protestants that the Church of the Holy Sepulchre carries for Catholics. And that may be true. But that does not diminish the feeling one has when one looks out at the skull staring back with macabre horror. It takes little imagination to recreate in one's mind the horrors of that Friday afternoon when the Son of God was put to death on a Roman gibbet with the world passing beneath him. Standing there today, looking out at the skull, I can understand why John records that one of the last things Jesus says, seeing his mother crumpled in grief at the foot of the cross, is, "John, take my mother home" (John 19:27).

The Scripture: John 19:17–30

So they took Jesus, and seizing his own cross he went out to what is called the Skull Place, which is called in Hebrew Golgotha, where they crucified him, and with him two others on either side, and Jesus between them. And Pilate also wrote a title and put [it] upon the cross; it read, "Jesus the Nazarene, the King of the Jews." And many of the Jews read this title, for the place where Jesus was crucified was near the city; and it was inscribed in Hebrew, Latin, and Greek. Therefore, the chief priests of the Jews said to Pilate, "Don't write 'the King of the Jews,' but rather, 'That man said, "I am the King of the Jews."'" Pilate answered, "What I have written I have written."

Then, the soldiers, when they crucified Jesus, took his clothes and made four parts, a part for each soldier, and also his tunic. But the tunic was seamless, woven from the top through the whole [garment]. And so they said to one another, "Let us not tear it; rather, let us cast lots for it [to see] whose it will be." This was so the scripture might be fulfilled that says, "They divided my garments among them, and for my clothing they cast lots." So the soldiers did these things.

But his mother, and his mother's sister, Mary [the wife] of Clopas, and Mary the Magdalene were standing by Jesus' cross. When Jesus saw his mother and the disciple whom he loved standing nearby, he said to [his] mother, "Woman, behold your son." Then, he said to the disciple, "Behold your mother." And from that hour the disciple took her home.

After this, Jesus, knowing that all things were now completed, in order that scripture might be fulfilled, said, "I thirst." A vessel full of vinegar was there; so, having put a sponge full of vinegar on hyssop, they put it up to his mouth. And when Jesus received the vinegar, he said, "It is finished," and lowering his head, gave up the spirit.

"The Letter"

I have always loved stories. I guess that's why I have always been drawn to good storytellers. Through the years my favorite storyteller has been the late Bennett Cerf. I used to love the old television program *To Tell the Truth,* mostly because of the possibility that Bennett Cerf, one of the panelists from time to time, might begin the show with one of his patented stories. He was a master of the pregnant pause. Of all the stories he told, this one, I guess, is still my favorite.[1]

A little girl whose parents died when she was quite young was bounced around from orphanage to foster home to orphanage. She really was a beautiful child, although all the trauma of moving and relocation took its toll on her fragile little ego. In time, she became quite withdrawn and introverted, retreating into a make-believe world populated by the only residents whom she felt she could trust without fear, the animal world—birds, squirrels, chipmunks, rabbits. Indeed, so shy and withdrawn did she become with people that she almost gave up speaking to people altogether. She would, however, be seen from time to time carrying on what appeared to be lively conversations with the little creatures that populated the grounds of the various orphanages in which she resided through so much of her formative years.

She finally came to live in a boarding house run by an older couple who managed the home not so much out of altruistic concern for the children who lived there as for the state welfare monies they collected for each child. Needless to say, the little girl became even more isolated and withdrawn. The only thing that kept her sane was her little friends, with whom she whiled away the hours.

Her very favorite was a certain squirrel that frolicked in the tree just outside her window. She would often go to the window and talk to the squirrel as though the animal could actually understand her, and a great bond soon developed between them.

One day, the woman who ran the orphanage went up to the little girl's room and found her talking to the squirrel through the open window. The woman flew into a rage. She scolded the little girl severely for encouraging silly animals to "hang around like that" and forbade her to do so again. With that, she slammed the window shut and stormed out of the room. But she didn't go far. Rather, she waited and listened at the door to see if the little girl would disobey her. When she heard no sound, she cracked the door and peered in. To her amazement, she saw the little girl busy at her worktable writing a note. The woman continued to watch her as she finished the note, put down the pencil, and then carefully folded the note in half. Then she got up and left the room with the note in hand.

The woman, now curious, followed the little girl as she went out of the house, through the yard, and up to the tree where her favorite squirrel usually stayed. She climbed up into the tree as far as she could, stretched out her little hand, and placed the note in the fork of two branches. Then, she climbed down and ran back up to her room.

The woman, puzzled and angry, summoned her husband to fetch the note from the tree. He did, and gave it to his wife to read. But when she read it, the anger in her face dissolved to shame. Her husband, curious, asked, "Well, what does it say?" And she gave it to him to read. He looked at it, and this is what he read: "To whoever finds this, I love you."

Two thousand years ago, on a dirty little hill at a busy crossroads just outside a major city in Palestine, between two crossed branches, God hung a letter. And it says, "To whoever finds this, I love you!"

But you knew that, didn't you? You knew that already.

For Further Discussion

1. Why did General Gordon believe that the rock cliff just north of the current Old City of Jerusalem was the place where Jesus had been crucified?
2. Crucifixion was not the only method of execution employed by the Romans. Why did they crucify people?
3. Both Gordon's Calvary and the Church of the Holy Sepulchre claim to be the place where Jesus was crucified. Which place seems more credible to you? Why?

NOTE

1. I heard Cerf tell this story years ago. If he has published it anywhere, I am unaware of it.

CHAPTER 14

The Garden Tomb

On the northeast side of Jerusalem's Old City, just outside the current walls, between Damascus Gate and Herod's Gate, lies one of the most beloved Christian sites in all Jerusalem: the Garden Tomb. The last remaining property that Great Britain retains from the period of the British Mandate (1918–1948), the Garden

Tomb is a serene, verdant oasis in the middle of the sights, sounds, and smells that assault the senses in the Old City of Jerusalem. The gardens, containing flora in a dizzying array, treat the eye to a palette of breathtaking color. Birds serenade visitors as they meander through the gardens. Groups of Christian pilgrims huddle under shade trees and sing songs of faith and celebrate Holy Communion, or just sit quietly reading their Bibles, praying, or reflecting on the significance of the crucifixion and resurrection for their faith. It's no wonder, then, that virtually everyone who makes the pilgrimage to the Holy Land calls this place their favorite.

But is it the place? Probably not. To be sure, John 19:41 says, "Now, there was in the place where he was crucified a garden, and in the garden a new tomb in which no one had ever been laid." The tour guides will point out to you that the skull-like escarpment that has come to be known as Gordon's Calvary (see chapter 13) is situated immediately adjacent to the gardens. Moreover, they will point out that, because of adequate irrigation produced from an elaborate underground cistern system, there has been a garden on that site for as long as anyone can remember. And they will point out to you in the garden an impressive, ancient tomb complex carved out of the limestone cliff, complete with a channel cut in the limestone for the rolling stone that was used, so they will say, to seal the tomb. But scholars will tell you that the area is too far removed from where the walled city of Jerusalem lay in Jesus' day, the current walls of the Old City dating only to the Moslem period (640–1099). Moreover, many scholars believe that the tomb to which the guides point as the tomb of Jesus dates only to the Byzantine period (324–640), as this particular type of tomb employed a burial trough arrangement typical of the Byzantine period, but not of the period of Jesus.[1] At this point, a brief discussion of first-century Jewish burial customs will be helpful.

In Palestine, death was an event that triggered certain compulsory rituals, necessitated partly by hygiene, partly by religious custom. Because of the hot climate, and because Jews, unlike Egyptians, didn't embalm corpses, bodies were buried on the same day the person died, the funeral typically being held within eight hours of death.[2] The body was bathed, rubbed with olive oil, and doused (anointed) with perfume. Then the body was wrapped in long strips of linen cloth, with aromatic spices (myrrh, aloe, etc.) being added between the cloth and the body to mask the smell of decaying flesh. The head was treated separately, being covered with its own linen napkin. While this was being done, family and friends gathered to mourn the deceased. Tearing their clothes as a sign of grief and donning dust and ashes to identify with the fate of the deceased, the mourners, often accompanied by flute players and professional women mourners, carried the body on a bier in sacred processional through the streets of the city to the place of burial.[3]

Often, the poor were buried in common, communal graves, such as the communal grave for paupers that can still be seen in the Kidron Valley near Jerusalem. More affluent persons were buried in tombs hewn out of the limestone rock that is everywhere in Palestine. In first-century Palestine, those tombs were typically of two different types: *kokim* or *arcosolia*. In both types, the opening in the limestone led into an antechamber surrounded by rock-hewn benches on which the body would be prepared for burial. Then, in the former type, the body would be placed to decompose in one of several horizontal shafts, called *kokim*. Other deceased family members would have occupied the other *kokim*. In the case of *arcosolia,* the body was placed on an arched-shaped ledge (*arco,* "arch" + *solium,* "sarcophagus") instead of in a shaft. The tomb was sealed by a large rolling stone and often whitewashed to warn Jews that a dead body was within so as to prevent potential defilement.[4] The body within was left to decompose ("sarcophagus" literally means "flesh eater"), with the bones being collected, once the decomposition process was complete, into a stone container called an ossuary.[5] Once the funeral was over, family members did no work for three days, and continued to mourn for a period of thirty days. Because the corpse had been in the family's house, the house was considered "unclean" for a period of time, preventing the preparation of food in the house. To obviate that concern, friends and neighbors prepared food for the mourning family during the time of the defilement. Our contemporary Christian practice of preparing food for grieving families no doubt derives from this tradition.

The tomb in the Garden Tomb is an *arcosolium,* having a trough rather than a ledge for the body. Whether it is the actual tomb of Joseph of Arimathea in which the body of Jesus was laid (cf. Mark 15:42–47 and parallels), no one can say for certain. Irrespective of its authenticity, it provides the pilgrim with a powerful picture of what the tomb of Jesus would have looked like.

The Scripture: John 19:38–20:18

And after this, Joseph of Arimathea, being a secret disciple of Jesus for fear of the Jews, asked Pilate in order that he might remove the body of Jesus. Pilate agreed. So he came and took his body. Then, Nicodemus also came, the one having come at first to [Jesus] by night, bearing a mixture of myrrh and aloe, about a hundred pounds' worth. Then,

they took the body of Jesus and bound it with linen cloths together with the spices, as is the burial custom of the Jews. Now in the place where he was crucified there was a garden, and in the garden a new tomb in which no one had ever been laid. Therefore, because the day of preparation [for Passover] of the Jews was near, and because the tomb was nearby, they laid Jesus there.

Then, on the first day of the week, Mary Magdalene came early, while it was still dark, to the tomb and saw the stone removed from the tomb. So she ran and came to Simon Peter and to the other disciple whom Jesus loved and said to them, "They've taken the Lord from the tomb, and we do not know where they've put him." Then Peter and the other disciple came out and went to the tomb. Both of them ran, but the other disciple ran ahead of Peter and came first to the tomb. And having stooped down, he peered inside [and saw] the linen cloths lying [there], but he did not enter. Then, Simon Peter also came, following him, and entered the tomb, and he saw the linen cloths lying [there], and the napkin, which had been over his head, lying not with the linen cloths, but apart, rolled up in one place. Then the other disciple, the one having come first to the tomb, entered, and he saw and believed. For not yet did they know the scripture that it is necessary for him to arise from the dead. Then the disciples departed again to their [homes].

But Mary stood outside the tomb weeping. Then, as she was crying, she stooped [to peer] into the tomb; and she saw two angels in white sitting, one at the head and one at the feet, where the body of Jesus had lain. And they said to her, "Woman, why are you crying?" She said to them, "[Because] they've taken my Lord, and I do not know where they've put him." Having said this, she turned around and saw Jesus standing, but she did not know that it was Jesus. Jesus said to her, "Woman, why are you crying? Whom do you seek?" She, supposing him to be the caretaker, said to him, "Sir, if you have removed him, tell me where you've put him, and I will take him." Jesus said to her, "Mary."

She, having turned, said to him in Hebrew, "Rabbouni" (which means Teacher). Jesus said to her, "Don't cling to me, for I have not yet ascended to my Father. Rather, go to my brothers and say to them, 'I ascend to my Father and your Father, my God and your God.'" Mary Magdalene left, proclaiming to the disciples, "I have seen the Lord," and [that] he said these things to her.

"Broken Things"

In a 1912 narrative poem titled "The Widow in the Bye Street," John Masefield tells the tragic story of Jimmy and his widowed mother, with whom he lives. They eke out a living in turn-of-the-century England by pooling their meager resources. She hems shrouds for the local undertaker; he works at the local quarry. But when Jimmy gets involved with Anna, a woman who turns out to have a dark, seamy side unknown to Jimmy, things begin to unravel. He catches her with another man and, in a fit of jealous rage, bashes his head in. Tried for murder, Jimmy is condemned to hang. Then, in a moving farewell scene, Masefield depicts the awful anguish of a grieving mother saying good-bye to her only son as he goes to the gallows. She laments:

> And God who gave His mercies takes His mercies.
> And God who gives beginning gives the end.
> I dread my death; but it's the end of curses,
> A rest for broken things too broke to mend.[6]

"Broken things," she muttered, "too broke to mend." Jesus' disciples would have understood those words on that awful Friday when Joseph of Arimathea, a secret disciple for fear of Jewish reprisal, laid the lifeless body of Jesus to rest in his own rock-hewn tomb. Peter and the others were nowhere to be found. Hiding out, no doubt, for fear that they'd be next, they cowered behind locked doors in dark corridors, hoping that it had all been just a bad dream.

"Was he dead?" one of them asked Simon.

"Well, he sure looked dead to me from where I was hid——, I mean, standing."

But then, something extraordinary happened. Early on Sunday, Mary Magdalene, and perhaps some other women with her, made her way out to the tomb to finish the job that Sabbath dusk had interrupted. But when she arrived at the tomb, the stone had been removed and the tomb was empty! She ran and called Simon and the other disciple, who ran to the tomb to see for themselves. And when they found Jesus' grave clothes but no body, they scratched their heads, looked at each other, and said, "Imagine that." And then, John says, they went home.

At first, it didn't even occur to them that God had been responsible for this. Mary first asked Simon and the other disciple, and then the caretaker of the cemetery, "What have they done with him? Have they no shame, desecrating a body like this?" But then, a voice behind her said, "Mary." And turning, she saw: there he was—alive! "Rabbouni!" she said, her mouth instinctively forming the name she had called him since first meeting him. "Don't hold me," he said.[7] "I haven't yet ascended to my Father. But go tell my brothers that I am ascending to my Father and to your Father, to my God and your God." This was no holy hallucination Mary had encountered. Bone and sinew were in her grasp. It was Jesus! He cast a shadow in the sunlight; he made noise when he walked.

And that, brothers and sisters, is the Christian hope. Not that anemic aspiration one often hears intoned at funerals: "For some things, there really is no death." That was the pagan hope, not the Christian's. Pagans, not Christians, believed that some things never really died. "Well, he's not really dead as long as I keep him alive in my memory." Indeed, much of our contemporary funerary practices are little more than pagan attempts to deny the reality of death.

"My, doesn't he look good!"

No. He looks dead.

I am reminded of a friend's response to well-meaning, but misguided, attempts at consolation at the death of his beloved wife. My friend had been in higher education for thirty years and was approaching retirement when his wife, the love of his life, suddenly died. Friends and colleagues attempted to console him by employing the traditional euphemisms of "death speak," such as "I'm sorry your wife passed away," or "I'm sorry to hear about your loss," or "I'm sorry that you've lost your wife." He responded by thanking his friends for their sympathies, but then informed them that, although well intentioned, their sentiments were impercipient. "My wife," he said, "didn't pass away. Nor did I lose my wife. I wouldn't be that careless with someone I loved. No. Make no mistake about it: my wife died. But as a Christian, I believe that that is not the last word about her. I believe in a God who brings dead things back to life again. And that is my hope, my only hope."

And that is the Christian hope, not that Jesus only seemed to be dead, or that some things never really die, or that death is powerless to kill love. Those are pagan hopes.

No. The Christian hope is that Jesus was dead—deader than a doornail—but God brought him back! Christians believe in a God who brings dead things to life again. God is a factor in the future, and with God there are no "broken things" that are "too broke to mend," no marriages, no families, no homes, no careers, no dreams. Easter has thrown "impossible" out of the lexicon of life. Isn't that true?

I heard about a seventy-four-year-old retired minister who, years ago while still active in parish ministry, became disillusioned, feeling that after having served all those many years as a pastor, he had made little difference in the lives of his parishioners. He calculated that in nearly forty years in the ministry in ten different churches, he had preached forty-two hundred sermons, and had ministered at four hundred funerals and two hundred weddings.

He decided to survey his former members to see what they remembered from nearly forty years of preaching. He discovered that they remembered almost nothing from all those sermons! (I have to say that I've never been tempted to do a survey like that. I've always assumed that it was my responsibility to tell you and that it was your responsibility to remember.) He was so disillusioned that he quit. He moved to a small town in northern Georgia, bought a little piece of land near the interstate highway, and planned to live out his days.

But then one day he heard a voice that he took to be the voice of God. "Howard," the voice said, "I want you to paint. I want you to put your visions of the world in pictures." Howard responded, "But I can't paint; I've never been trained to paint." The voice answered, "How do you know if you don't try!"

And so Howard started to paint, on everything—old hubcaps, Coke bottles, pieces of discarded plywood, a Delta Airlines baggage container. He even painted a landscape on the hood of an old, abandoned Cadillac. He *said* that he'd never been trained. Beautiful landscapes and still lifes began to appear on all kinds of junk that had been discarded on the roadside by his property, most with subtle Christian symbolism and imagery. Then, he started to sculpt. He created incredible collages out of all kinds of discarded junk—broken glass, old watches, bicycles, a mirror broken off a car. He fashioned a beautiful cruciform out of the handles of an old, discarded lawnmower.

Slowly, the junk was transformed into beauty. And then, he made a remarkable discovery: People were now *interested* in their junk. They would see his work while passing by on the highway and stop to admire it. After a while, so many began to stop to look at his art that he came up with the idea of creating a beautiful garden area that would give travelers a pleasant break. He planted gardens. He constructed paths. And all around, he placed his artwork. He called it "Paradise Garden," as a way of saying that God is at work in the world turning the wilderness we have created back into Eden.

And people began to stop by the hundreds to see his junk—broken watches and broken bicycles and broken cars and farm equipment (you can't see stuff like that at Disney World!)—all of it fashioned into things of beauty. It is the most beautiful collection of junk you've ever seen, all of it shaped with the message and the power of the love of God.

Right in the middle of "Paradise" is a sculpture on which is inscribed this poem:

I took the pieces you threw away,
I put them together by night and day,
Washed by the rain, dried by the sun,
A million pieces all in one,
To remind a broken world
What God can do
With what it's done.

Brothers and sisters, I know that a lot of things in your life right now seem broken—hopes, careers, marriages, families, health. And for some of you the future appears pretty bleak, nothing but "broken things, too broke to mend."

But there is also God. God is a factor in the future. And so, drag out all your broken things, your shattered dreams and broken toys, all the things you thought "too broke to mend." Because I have a Gospel word for you: Easter has happened! God raised Jesus from the dead, and that makes *everything* possible, doesn't it. Well, doesn't it?

For Further Discussion

1. Which site seems to be more authentic as the place of Jesus' resurrection, the Church of the Holy Sepulchre or the Garden Tomb? Why?

2. How do ancient Jewish burial and funerary practices compare with modern ones?

3. How much of contemporary Christian funerary practices actually reflect pagan, rather than Christian, values and beliefs? What alternative traditions would more truly reflect our faith?

4. If the Christian hope is not so much in the belief that some things never really die, but that God brings dead things to life again, how should Christians comfort one another in grief?

5. Why did Mary Magdalene fail to recognize the risen Jesus in the garden?

NOTES

1. See Jack Finegan, *The Archeology of the New Testament: The Life of Jesus and the Beginning of the Early Church* (Princeton, N.J.: Princeton University Press), 173.

2. See Peter Connolly, *Living in the Time of Jesus of Nazareth* (Oxford: Oxford University Press, 1983), 60.

3. Matthew 9:23 reflects this custom: "And Jesus, having come to the house of the ruler and seeing the flute players and the crowd making a commotion. . . ."

4. Recently, one scholar has argued that the covering stone was not a "rolling stone," but a square or rectangular stone that was slid, rather than rolled, in front of the entrance. See Amos Kloner, "Did a Rolling Stone Close Jesus' Tomb?" *Biblical Archaeological Review* 25, no. 5 (1999): 23–24. For a New Testament reference to "white-washed tombs," see Matthew 23:27.

5. The practice of collecting the bones of deceased family members into a family ossuary is rather colorfully described in the Old Testament as "gathering the bones to the fathers." See Genesis 49:29 and Judges 2:10.

6. John Masefield, "The Widow in the Bye Street," in *Poems by John Masefield* (New York: Macmillan, 1941), 186.

7. The familiar King James Version of Jesus' words to Mary in John 20:17 obscures and misleads the intent of the text. Biblical Greek has two ways to prohibit an action: a "prohibitive subjunctive," which prohibits an action from ever beginning; and a "prohibitive imperative," which stops an action already in progress. The King James Version translates Jesus' words *mē mou haptou* as though they were a prohibitive subjunctive, "Touch me not!" when in fact they are a prohibitive imperative, "Stop holding on to me!"

Appendix

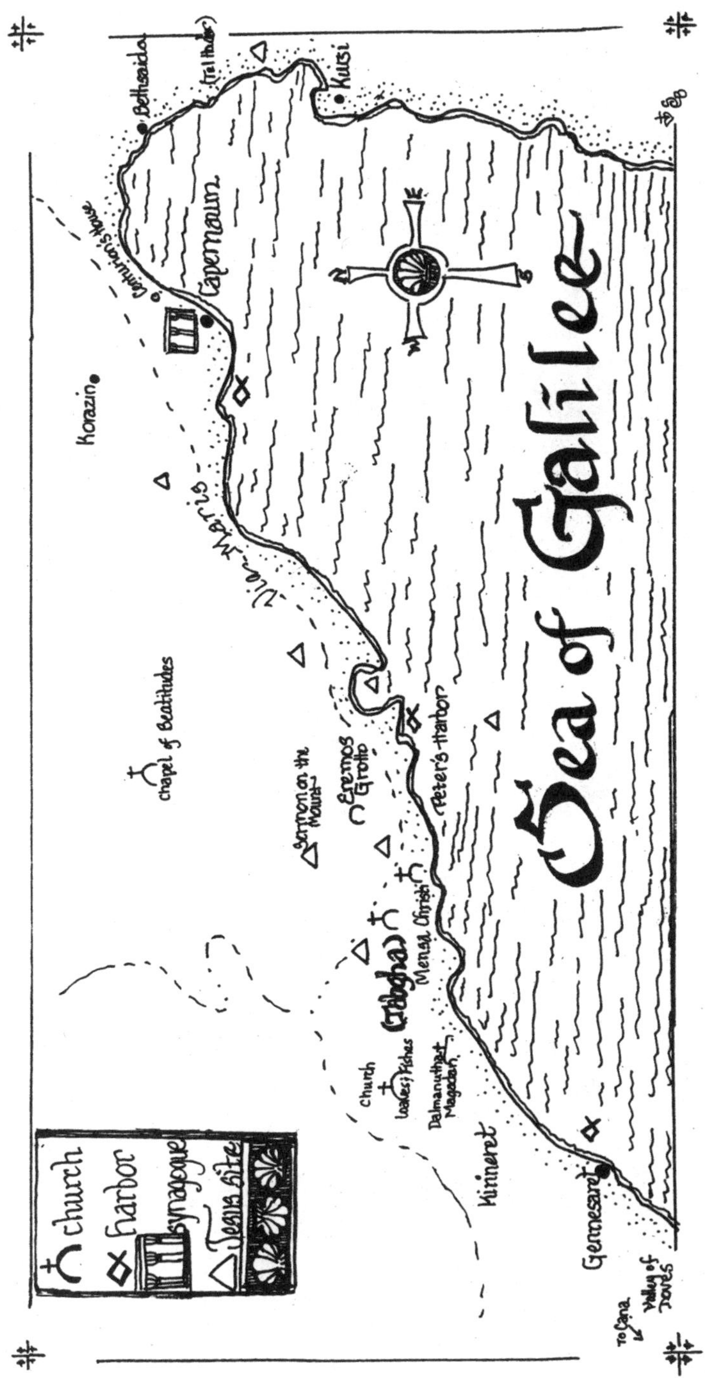
church
harbor
synagogue
Jesus site
Sea of Galilee
Bethsaida
Kursi
Capernaum
Centurion's House
Korazin
Via Maris
Chapel of Beatitudes
Sermon on the Mount
Eremos Grotto
Peter's Harbor
Mensa Christi
Church
Loaves & Fishes
Kinneret
Gennesaret
To Cana
Valley of Doves

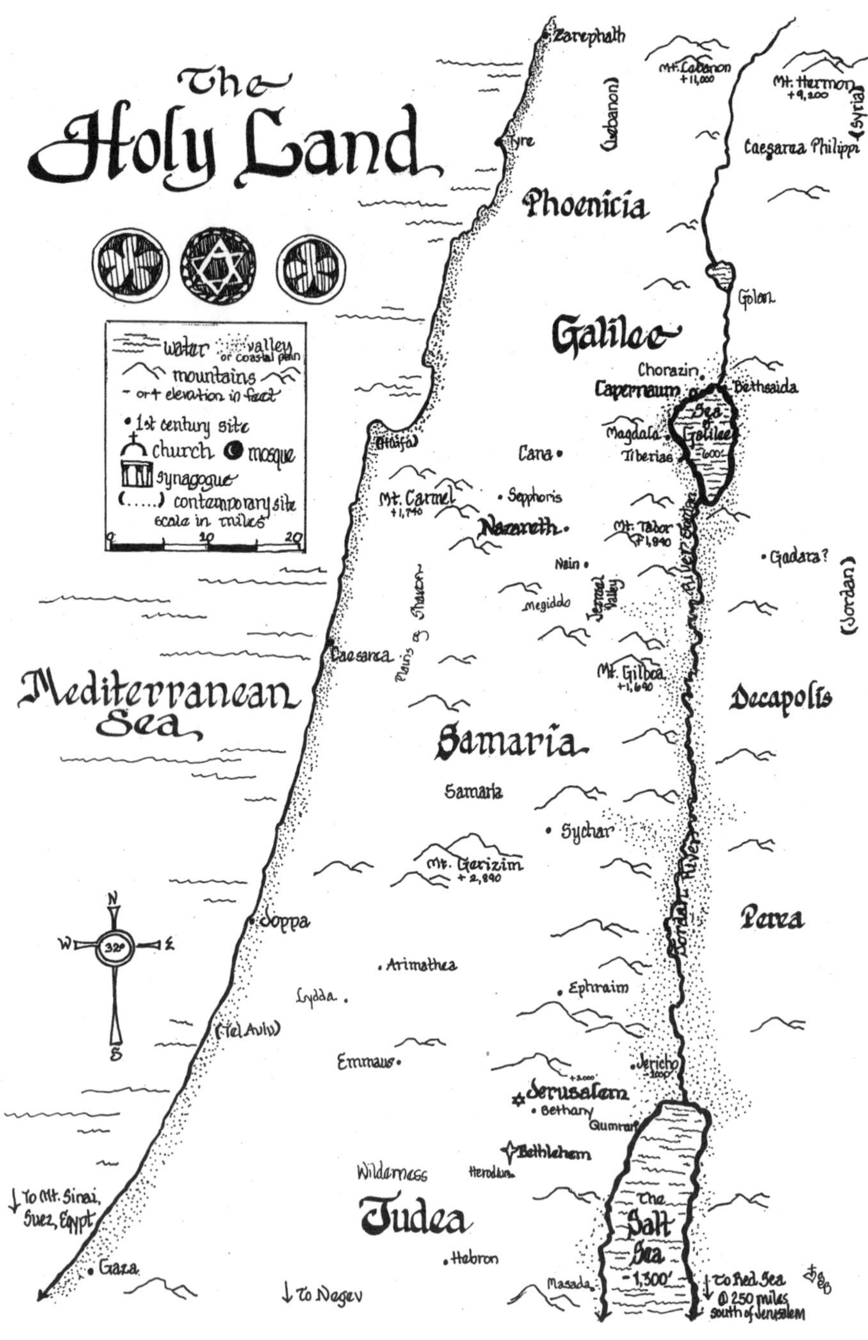
The Holy Land
water
valley or coastal plain
mountains
- or + elevation in feet
1st century site
church
mosque
synagogue
(.....) contemporary site
scale in miles
0 10 20
Zarephath
Mt. Lebanon +11,000
Mt. Hermon +9,200
(Syria)
(Lebanon)
Tyre
Caesarea Philippi
Phoenicia
Golan
Galilee
Chorazin
Capernaum
Bethsaida
Sea of Galilee
-600'
Magdala
Tiberias
Cana
(Haifa)
Mt. Carmel +1,740
Sepphoris
Nazareth
Mt. Tabor +1,840
Nain
Gadara?
(Jordan)
Megiddo
Jezreel Valley
Plains of Sharon
Caesarea
Mt. Gilboa +1,690
Decapolis
Mediterranean Sea
Samaria
Samaria
Sychar
Mt. Gerizim +2,890
Jordan River
Perea
N
W
32°
E
S
Joppa
Arimathea
Lydda
Ephraim
(Tel Aviv)
Emmaus
+3,000'
Jericho -1000'
Jerusalem
Bethany
Qumran
Bethlehem
Herodium
Wilderness
Judea
The Salt Sea
-1,300'
Hebron
Masada
To Mt. Sinai, Suez, Egypt
Gaza
To Negev
To Red Sea @ 250 miles south of Jerusalem

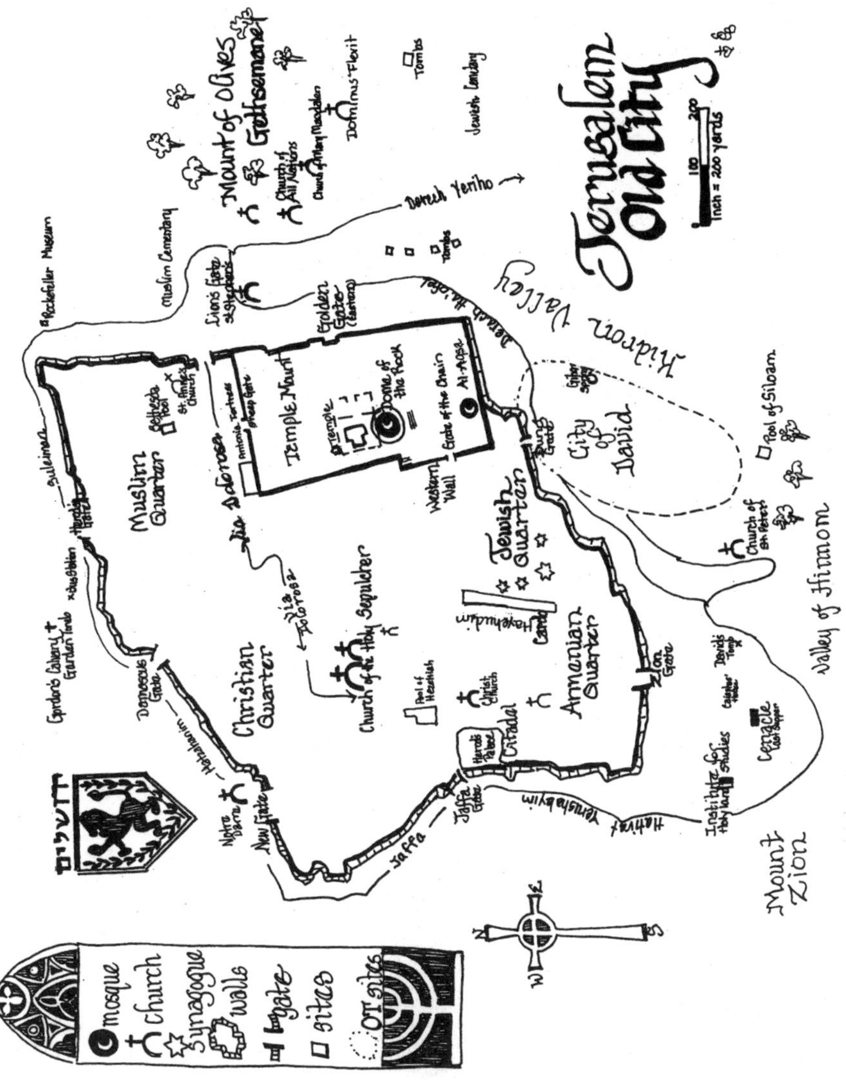

Jerusalem
Old City
1 inch = 200 yards
Muslim Quarter
Christian Quarter
Jewish Quarter
Armenian Quarter
Temple Mount
Dome of the Rock
Al-Aqsa
Western Wall
Via Dolorosa
Church of the Holy Sepulcher
Citadel
Jaffa Gate
Zion Gate
Damascus Gate
New Gate
Herod's Gate
Lion's Gate
Golden Gate
Dung Gate
City of David
Kidron Valley
Valley of Hinnom
Mount Zion
Mount of Olives
Gethsemane
Dominus Flevit
Muslim Cemetery
Jewish Cemetery
Tombs
Rockefeller Museum
Derech Yeriho
Pool of Siloam
Church of St. Peter
Cenacle
David's Tomb
Pool of Hezekiah
Christ Church
Notre Dame
Gordon's Calvary Garden Tomb
Church of All Nations
Church of St. Mary Magdalen
mosque
church
synagogue
walls
gate
sites
OT sites

NOTES

NOTES